UNIVERSITY RESEARCH MONOGRAPHS
Number 12.

THE SCHOOL IN
AMERICAN LITERATURE

THE SCHOOL IN
AMERICAN LITERATURE

BY
RICHARD ALLEN FOSTER

BALTIMORE
WARWICK AND YORK, INC.
1930

Copyright, 1930, by
Warwick & York, Inc.

———

Printed in the United States of America

———

The Maple Press Company, York, Pa.

CONTENTS

ACKNOWLEDGMENTS

Sincere thanks are due to the librarians of Columbia University and of Teachers College for assistance in procuring books; to my wife for her unlimited pains in typing the manuscript and in proof reading; to Professor Allan Abbott who not only read the manuscript but who always generously and kindly gave help and encouragement; to Professor Edward H. Reisner and to Professor Ralph L. Rusk who made constructive suggestions of great value; to Professor Roy Hiram Wilson of Ohio University and Professor J. Duncan Spaeth of Princeton University who were interested and encouraging advisers; and to Professor William C. Bagley for his interest and practical assistance in the matter of publication.

To Professor Franklin T. Baker I owe not only the original suggestion of this study but countless suggestions patiently given both in his English Seminar and in the many hours of pleasant conference with him.

THE SCHOOL IN AMERICAN LITERATURE

CHAPTER I

INTRODUCTORY: THE SCHOOL AS A LITERARY THEME

The school is as old as civilization. Long before the Hebrew child had uttered his "precept upon precept and line upon line," or before the patriarchal "train-up-a-child-in-the-way-he-should-go" had become a proverb, it was. Even in the beginning was the word and this word became the foundation of the school.

As an institution old traditions and associations have hovered about it lovingly, and these are the stuff of poetry. Who has not heard of a Teacher who took his pupils up to a mountain for private instruction? Or who has not heard of Shakespeare's "whining schoolboy with his satchel and shining morning face," or Chaucer's "litel clergyeon seven year of age," or his clerk of Oxenford who would gladly learn and gladly teach; or Heywood's "To tell tales out of school;" or Goldsmith's "joyful children just let loose from school;" or Dr. Johnson's

> "There mark what ills the scholar's life assail
> Toil, envy, want, the patron and the jail;"

1

or Lamb's "In my joyful schooldays, in my days of childhood;" or Byron's "Schoolboy's tale, the wonder of an hour;" or Whittier's

> "Still sits the schoolhouse on the hill,
>   A ragged beggar sunning."

Ghostlike we pace round the haunts of our childhood, seeking to find "the old familiar faces." So it is the old familiar things quarried from the bed-rock of human nature that find a place most readily in literature and art.

The school then has long been known in song and story from the epigrams of Martial[1] to the poems of Whittier. It forms a chief experience in the life of every man whether it be one of Shakespeare's seven ages or one of Solomon Grundy's seven days. Again as Shakespeare made famous the comparison of the world with the stage, so Crabbe and Franklin called the world a school, Franklin adding emphatically that fools will learn in no other.[2] Not long after Crabbe and Franklin, Disraeli wrote of "the microcosm of a public school,"[3] and today we frequently hear such a comparison made with the college. It is then a little world—a world full of ambition and defeat, courage, hope and despair, friendship, love and hatred which are the substances of life; and if of life of art, for art is life. Here, as in the treatment of life, the battle has gone on between the romanticist and the realist, some men idealizing the school, others satirizing it. It is now no longer looked upon so much

[1] About A.D., 40–104. See poetical translation of Martial's "Schoolmaster" by Paul Nixon in *Century Readings in Ancient Classical Literature*, Showerman, 521.

[2] *Crabbe Poems* (London, 1834) Vol. VI, 47. "We name the world a school."

[3] Disraeli, *Vivian Grey* (Philadelphia, 1850) Chapter I, 6.

as a preparation for life, but as life itself. In poetry this is true even in the days when it was regarded as a step in getting ready to live, though at that time it was under severe conventional restraints. For who does not often "in lonely rooms 'mid the din of towns and cities, when the fretful stir unprofitable and the fever of the world" hang upon him, remember with joy the whipping he had at school; or the part he took in the *barring out?* He who has not "played hookey" from its restraints and idled away the long afternoon with companions in some sunny spot of the deep forest or on the slippery bank of some yellow swimming hole, or who has not taken his "blamed old willer pole" and "made tracks" for the hole where the sun fish wait, has not known the pleasures of being a boy at school.

This whole question of the school in literature is bound up with associations and memories of town and country life as well as, more recently, with the more complex life of the city. At the time the first settlements were being made in America and through the eighteenth and nineteenth centuries the school was developing as a European tradition in literature, though at times its treatment was fragmentary. Chaucer used it in *The Prioresses Tale* sketching briefly child life at a medieval church school with consummate art. In the pageantry of human life as portrayed by Shakespeare the schoolmaster is not omitted, and in one case when Mistress Ann Page asks Sir Hugh Evans to test her son's progress in his accidence a concrete illustration of a contemporary school recitation in Latin grammar is given.[1] In *Love's Labor's Lost* he satirizes in the gayest fashion the pedantry, puerility, affectation, and euphuism which were rampant during Elizabeth's reign . . . "herself the most

[1] *Merry Wives of Windsor*, Act IV, Sc. I.

affected and detestable of the euphuists."[1]   Roger
Ascham, John Milton, Francis Bacon, and Thomas
Fuller—all dealt with the school in a more philosophical
manner.   Their works in English, however, are better
known as literary monuments than as educational
documents.   Dean Swift in describing the Academy at
Lagodo in *Gulliver's Travels* (1726) and Pope in *The
Dunciad* (1742) denounce most bitterly in imaginative
literature the pedagogical practices of the time.

By far the most notable and extended treatment of
school life in eighteenth century England is Shenstone's
Schoolmistress (1737) the heroine of which "boasts unruly
brats to tame."   Though he gives a very sympathetic
portrait of the old dame and her brood of scholars, he
strikes an emphatic blow at the weakness of brutal discipline as a corrective measure.   "Beware, ye dames,—ye
quench not too the sparks of nobler fires."   Cowper's
poem, *Tirocinium, or A Review of Schools* (1784), on the
other hand, written for the purpose of recommending private rather than public education, repeats Dr. Johnson's
dictum that with less flogging there is always less learning.
George Crabbe (1754–1832) in *the Parish Register* (1807)
and in *The Borough* (1810) paints sternly and uncompromis-
ingly the school life of the community in which he was
born.   The variety of schools described in *The Borough*—
Dame Schools, Day Schools, Schools for Ladies, and *Boarding Schools for Boys*—suggests not only a larger and more
complex society than the village of Shenstone's poem but
a growing interest in education in general.

In addition to the three English poets mentioned who
have treated the school intensively, Goldsmith, Prior,
Burns, and Byron, all have given notable vignettes of

[1] Green, *History of the English People* (N. Y., 1916), 400.   See
also *Britannica Encyclopedia*, "Elizabeth," by Walter Raleigh.

the life, but their chief interest, too, was in the school-master or schoolmistress, or educational theory and disci-pline. Only Shenstone, Goldsmith, and Crabbe attempt to construct an idyllic picture of the subject, and even they are not free from pedagogical theorizing. As the interest in children set in motion by the great reformers of eighteenth century France and England increases, literary artists turn increasingly to various phases of child life, of which the school is one. It was, therefore, in the nineteenth century that the school became established as a theme in English and American litera-ture. Then it was, too, that Hughes' *Tom Brown's Schooldays*, De Amicis' *Cuore*, and Kipling's *Stalky and Co.*, built out of the imperishable material of boylife, emerged.

In general the writers of America have followed the conventions of the Old World in seeking literary themes; hence the literature dealing with the school in America is inevitably connected with the classicism of the seven-teenth and eighteenth centuries and with the romanticism of the nineteenth century which are, in turn, involved with the growth of democracy and the education of the masses. It is noteworthy that English literature pre-vious to the nineteenth century shows neglect of the com-mon people if not contempt for them. "Shakespeare was *of* us, Milton was *for* us, Burns, Shelley were *with* us." Browning's varying use of the preposition reveals the trend of affairs. Since the literature of the common people was little known previous to Burns and Shelley, there was not much literature dealing with school life except to reflect its brutal discipline and gerund-grinding formality. Not until after Dickens (1812–1871) had assisted in breaking the chains of these two taskmasters, did any considerable change come in the use of the school as literary material. From Pope to Wordsworth as long as poetry was formal and didactic, the school remained a prominent subject for poetry, for it lent itself conveniently to satirical and essay-like structure.

That the literary theologians and versifiers of early America did not see many possibilities in the school as a theme is no more than is to be expected; education was subordinate to the church and weighed down with moral inculcations. If clergymen were in the saddle, however, they paid due respect to worthy schoolmasters in an occasional eulogy or elegy. Probably not until the end of the eighteenth century can it be said that America came into belles-lettres, and in the first flaring up of literary culture among the Hartford Wits, education was reviewed as *The Progress of Dulness*. When, after the Revolution, imaginative authors sought for material, they found the fresh substances in the life of the Indians, in the flora and fauna of the New World as well as its new institutions more attractive than the highly conventional life of the schoolroom.[1]

There was, however, an ardent zeal to know among the Puritans, "a passion for improvement" Irving somewhat satirically called it,[2] and this zeal expressed itself in their passing of laws and making provision for education. Hence a great body of crude technical literature has developed along with the history of education in America which has given utterance to this enthusiasm. But with the development of the district system in New England, a certain literary flavor became associated with "the little red schoolhouse" and has persisted in our literature for more than a hundred years. Likewise with the growth of boarding schools for boys and girls, school

[1] *Cambridge History of American Literature*, Vol. III, 423–424.
[2] *Knickerbocker History* (N. Y., 1865), 224.

stories have become as popular as the advertisements of these schools in the leading magazines. Of recent years high schools and the complex school life of the great city systems have found someone to tell their story. So popular have these stories become with children themselves, that together with Boy and Girl Scout Stories they have almost supplanted the dime dreadfuls of a generation ago. No longer does the old schoolmaster hold his place in the limelight, but the substance of boy life— athletics, fleetness of foot, physical beauty and prowess, loyalty to one's school, camaraderie, admiration for natural ability, and a contempt for the plodder—make up the salient features of the contemporary school story. When these stories first began to appear, there were death-bed heroics, rescues from burning buildings and highly-colored moral crises, but more recent writers have made an attempt to come into a sympathetic understanding of child life.

Perhaps the chief reason for the prominence of school stories in America is the general tendency of the people to idealize education. Few, indeed, have been the instances in our literary history where this material has been touched by genius, but these have been sufficient to reflect the relation of the schoolmaster and his school to life. It is the purposes of the chapters that follow to trace the emergence of the school into *imaginative* American literature in the light of our educational and literary history and of the growing interest in childhood. The word school, though of wide meaning in literature, is here taken to mean not merely a place for instruction, but an institution of a teacher or teachers and learners, including only elementary and secondary education.

Chapter II

THE IDEALIZATION OF EDUCATION IN AMERICA

In America no literature of any importance was produced before the nineteenth century. The seventeenth century was occupied with colonizing, with the struggle of the colonies with each other and with the Indians, and with the establishment of English supremacy in America. By 1800 we had won political independence from England, but the States had not yet been firmly knit together and the form of government was still an experiment. The literature up to this time was, properly speaking, English literature, for not only were its ideas, ideals, and forms products of the mother country, but the majority of writers were Englishmen living in America.[1] These men, however, could not live so far from the home land without responding to the new environment. Though we look for the sources of our civilization on the other side of the water, though, as Barrett Wendell says, "The ideals which underlie our conscious life must always be the ideals which underlie the conscious life of the mother country,"[2] yet the emphasis given to those ideals in the new environment may be very different.

This fact may be observed in the general tendency to idealize education in America. Whatever may be said

[1] One of the influences which welded the countries inseparably together was the King James Version of the Bible, 1611.

Cf. Jas. H. Smart, *The Schools of Indiana* (Cincinnati, 1876), 22.

[2] Wendell, *Literary History of America* (N. Y., 1900), 5.

of the economic pressure in southeast England that forced the Puritans to come to this country,[1] it is a commonplace of history that the purpose of their coming was an ideal one.[2] The traditional Englishman is said to have believed in the dictum, "Whatever is, is right;" the Puritans, on the other hand, were not satisfied with things as they were, but set about to fashion a new world as they thought it ought to be. In this work John Robinson, Bradford, Winthrop, Brewster, and a host of university men were the leading spirits. "It is possible," says Tyler, "that between the years 1630 and 1690 there were in New England as many graduates of Cambridge and Oxford as could be found in any population of similar size in the mother country." Miss Crawford points out that Cambridge was the cradle of the Puritan idea, for the people of East Anglia had early been endowed by the *poor priests* with Wyclifian thought. Robinson and Brewster were both products of Cambridge; Brewster became soon after graduation an assistant to Queen Elizabeth's Secretary of State, Sir William Davison, and, upon losing his position, went back to Scrooby to found the Puritan church there. These men certainly were not afraid of venturing something for an ideal.

While the differences between the settlers in Virginia and New England have been magnified, it seems probable

[1] The exodus to Holland was due to economic pressure largely. See Channing, *History of United States*, Vol. I, Chapter X. See also Beard, Charles and Mary, *The Rise of the American Civilization* (N. Y., 1927), Chapter II.

[2] Fiske, *The Beginning of New England*, Chapters I–III.

Eggleston, *The Transit of Civilization*, Chapters I–II.

Tyler, M. C., *History of American Literature*, Vol. I, 96–98.

Crawford, Mary C., *In the Days of the Pilgrim Fathers*, Chapters I–IV.

Morton, Nathaniel, "*New England's Memorial*" in Masefield's *Chronicles of the Pilgrim Fathers*, Everyman Edition, 7–17.

that the greater difference may be found in the zeal of the Puritans to know. John Adams writing in his "Diary" for July 21, 1786, throws light on this zeal as well as the difference between the two colonies. "Major Langbourne dined with us again. He was lamenting the difference of character between Virginia and New England. I offered to give him a receipt for making a New England in Virginia. He desired it; and I recommended to him town-meetings, training days, *town-schools*, and ministers." Here were four things the Puritans honored, and not the least of these is the idea of town schools. It amounted with them to little less than reverence. "Probably no other community of pioneers ever so honored study, so reverenced the symbols and instruments of learning," writes Tyler. It is not surprising, then, that universal education should seem to them a universal necessity and that they should provide for it in all grades. This was a strong factor in establishing the tradition in America that any child or person who has a desire and capacity for an education should not be denied the chance of schooling. "If a boy in any country village," writes Lowell, "showed uncommon parts, the clergyman was sure to hear of it. He and the squire and the doctor, if there was one, talked it over, and the boy was sure to be helped onward to college; for next to the five points of Calvinism our ancestors believed in a college education; that is, in the best education that could be secured. Ah! how the parents—nay the whole family—moiled and pinched that their boy might have the chance denied to them."[1]

That Harvard should be founded in the days when the colony was poverty-stricken is evidence of Massachusetts' intellectual vigor. Speaking of a much later

[1] Lowell's Works (Boston, 1910), Vol. II, 10–12.

time when New England had grown in stature and wisdom, George Herbert Palmer says: "In the Puritan home there was the insistence on learning, fostered by the presence of abundant books, by studies around the center table, by reading aloud that went on whenever three or four could be gathered together."[1] Lavish expense was incurred and stringent economy practiced for it.

That little fiction was read in the Puritan home until the middle of the nineteenth century is doubtless true; but this fact does not prove a hostility to poetry, music, and the fine arts in general. Palmer, who has himself idealized teaching, records that his grandfather was a lover of Pope; that his mother and father both wrote respectable verse; that he was named for his clerical uncle's favorite poet—George Herbert. The poems of Burns were printed in America two years after their appearance in Scotland (1786) and the *Lyrical Ballads* four years after its appearance in England. Goodrich records that his father's favorite poets were King David and Dr. Watts; that he was an excellent reader; that he read the Bible through to the family thirteen times in twenty-five years in "a clear, frank hearty voice."[2] The passion for improvement was bound up in the heart of every true Puritan. Franklin, though breaking from Bostonian restraints, carried some of the inheritance from New England soil with him. In his *Proposal Relating to the Education in Pennsylvania* (1749),[3] he declares that the "good education of youth has been esteemed by wise men

[1] Palmer, George Herbert, "The Puritan Home," ATLANTIC MONTHLY, Vol. 128, page 391.

[2] Goodrich, *Recollections* (N. Y., 1856), Vol. I, 157–164.

[3] U. S. Bureau of Education, Circular No. 2, Washington, 1892, 58–63.

in all ages as the surest foundation of happiness both of private families and of commonwealths." He glows with enthusiasm at the prospect of the culture of young minds, quoting from Thomson:

> When infant reason grows apace and calls,
> For the kind hand of an assiduous care;
> Delightful task! to rear the tender thought
> To teach the young idea how to shoot;
> To pour the fresh instruction o'er the mind,
> To breathe the enlivening spirit and to fix
> The generous purpose in the glowing breast.[1]

Accordingly the constitution of the Public Academy which he sought to found in the city of Philadelphia began: "Nothing can more effectively contribute to the cultivation and improvement of a country, the Wisdom, Riches and Strength, Virtue and Piety, the Welfare and Happiness of a people, than a proper Education of Youth, by forming their manners, imbuing their tender minds with Principles of Rectitude and morality"[2] . . .

What does not change in the Puritan wherever found is the "immortal urgent spirit that breaks from old forms, follows the new vision, seriously seeks the discipline of the higher life."[3] "Build thee more stately mansions, Oh my soul" were words uttered from the heart of him. He, too, would "rather be put to death many times than to call a pin a point or speak the least against his understanding;" that is why he made his final appeal from the letter to the spirit of the Scripture.[4] It is largely in this fact that we find the explanation of the Unitarian

[1] Ibid., 58–59.

[2] Facsimile of original draft of the charter. Ibid., opposite page 62.

[3] Sherman, Stuart P., ATLANTIC MONTHLY, Vol. 128, page 349.

[4] Ibid., 350.

and the transcendental movements. Not many generations of such men were required to produce an Emerson, who was to idealize both education and independent scholarship in enduring language. The world, says he, is "man's teacher, and only teacher."[1] Sun, moon, plant, and animal exist only to arouse his interior activity. Both necessity and man's love of power are the teaching forces. He becomes a part of all he meets, the end of life being that man should take the universe into himself and realize the infinitude of his own consciousness. This is the business of education, to awaken the child to the world and to himself. To take on dogmatism is to renounce the search for truth. The word "education," is itself dogmatic and cold—a mere convention for true education; it "affects us with a certain yawning of the jaws." Even when the law touches it, we are not to take it for granted that it shall be accomplished; for education is as broad as man. Its aim should be not only to make attorneys and engineers; but to make an able, earnest, great-hearted man. Though Emerson held that education should inflame youth toward the "Great Mind in which he lives," his feet were firmly enough set on Yankee soil for him to add that such zeal should not monopolize the youth completely.

It is a low self-love in the parent, he continues, for him to wish his child to repeat his character and fortune. "Can we not let people be themselves? . . .You are trying to make that child another you. One's enough." God is forever invading the old dead world with a new, young soul, and it must be respected. We must teach each child with a believing and prophetic eye, remem-

[1] Emerson, R. W., *Essay on Education* (Houghton, Boston, 1883). *The American Scholar* (Boston, 1837).

bering that the "world is needed for his tuition." There is no such thing as mass education; it must be done reverently, one by one. Do not lose your love for learning in the routine of grammars and books of elements. School authorities like to lay down curricula in order that such specific things as writing, grammar, and arithmetic may be taught. They wish to formalize education. But for heaven's sake "smuggle in a little contraband wit, fancy, imagination, and thought." Here is education, idealized and transcendentalized.

Such a desire to discover *Nature* and the world for one's self as found in Emerson's Essays represents the flowering of the Puritan educational ideal, an ideal which has been expressed not only in literature but in the spread of popular education. It was reflected in American travel literature of the eighteenth and nineteenth centuries;[1] it was expressed in Franklin's passion to know, and in the stream of American graduates that entered German universities after 1815. "Child," said an early New England mother to her boy, "if God make thee a good Christian and a good scholar thou hast all thy mother ever asked for thee."[2] It is just this zeal for religion that in one way accounts for the idealization of education. The Puritan mother and father felt, perhaps vaguely, that education could save the souls of their children. Even in Virginia (1691) the Reverend James

---

[1] Rochefoucault, *Travels in America* (London, 1799), Chapter I, 530.

Frederika Bremer, *America of the Fifties* (N. Y., 1924), 19, 95, 283, 286, 315, 317.

[2] Tyler, New York, 1878, Vol. I, 100. Compare the words of Tom Brown's father. *Tom Brown's School days*, London, 1857.

"If he'll only turn out a brave, helpful and truth telling Englishman, and a gentleman, and a Christian, that's all I want," said Squire Brown of Lorn when Tom started away to Rugby.

Blair, in sending to England a plea for funds to build a college, explained to Attorney General Seymour that his people had souls to be saved. But the reply from the homeland was, "Damn your souls. Raise tobacco."[1]

Though in New England some had to be reminded that their taxes were over-due, and though the early Almanacs repeatedly satirize the farmer for employing incompetent teachers, this condition was aside from the general tendency to surround education with a glamor. Puritan wives and mothers, it is true, felt the cultural value of education more than the fathers. Farmers who sent their sons to academies were often urged to do so by wives and mothers who felt somehow that the boys' souls would be saved by it. So distinctly did this religious zeal in education develop that during the first half of the nineteenth century publishers took advantage of it and the markets were flooded with books and periodicals that made the "Christian appeal."[2] If we are to believe the testimony of autobiographical fiction, fathers, though proud of the free public school system, were likely to have an eye to taxes and costs and to think that reading, writing, and ciphering were sufficient for sons who were to follow in their footsteps on the farm, while, on the other hand, mothers kept the religious and cultural values constantly in mind.[3] The ideals of the ministry still remained as an important factor in education, even after it was secularized. The horn-book and the catechism influenced *The New England Primer;* and the *New England Primer*, *Webster's Speller* and the subsequent school readers. From each letter of the alphabet

[1] Sparks, *Franklin*, Vol. X, 111.
[2] Williams, *Our Rural Heritage* (N. Y., 1925), 36–40.
[3] Thompson, *Locke Amsden* (Boston, 1890), 16, 30, 45–46.

in the *New England Primer*, some divine truth was to emanate:

> Z——Zaccheus he
> Did climb the tree
> His Lord to see

is the jingle that ends the alphabet. Even through the alphabet children were to get "Spiritual Milk drawn from the breasts of both Testaments for their souls' nourishment."

If early education strove to make little Zaccheuses out of youth, it also strove to frighten them with the devil and his brood. How this form of idealization is involved with the idea of the Puritan Hell is seen in the "Dialogue between Christ, Youth and the Devil" in the *New England Primer*, which is a kind of *Sinner-in-the-Hand-of-an-Angry-God* sermon for children. Youth resolves to spend his time in sport and play—a resolution which makes the devil very happy. He says if youth will learn to shun the ways of grace and truth and learn to lie, to curse, fight, scratch "and also bite," to pout and be sullen, and to disobey his parents, he would be the child for him.

> When others Read, be thou at play,
> Think not on God, don't sigh nor pray;
> Nor be thou such a silly fool,
> To mind thy book, or go to school;
> But play the truant, fear not, I
> Will help thee straightway to a Lie,
> Which will excuse thee from the same—
> ——Come bow to me.

Christ urges Youth not to make such a choice: "Grant me thy heart, and thy joys shall last eternally." Youth says, "Not for me." He cannot set his mind on sorrows and heavy crosses. Christ then tells him that he will give him wholly to Satan who will harden his heart in sin. Then

> In ire I'll cut thee down————
> In Hell at last thy soul must burn.

The youth being frightened, exclaims that he will turn to Christ and give up all thought of pleasure. The devil urges him not to change his mind; Christ tells him it is now too late, for

"I in thy youth grim Death will send."

Death then appears, at the tragic moment saying:

> Youth I am come to fetch thy Breath,
> And carry thee to the shades of Death,
> No pity on thee I can show,
> Thou hast thy God offended so.
> Thy Soul and Body I'll divide,
> Thy Body in the Grave I'll hide,
> And thy dear Soul in Hell must lye
> With Devils to Eternity;
> Thus ends the Days of woeful Youth,
> Who won't obey, nor mind the Truth.
> Nor harken to what *Preachers say*,
> But their *Preachers disobey*.

Thus it was to outwit the "old deluder Satan," that the order of the General Court in the Colony of Massachusetts Bay in 1647 was carried out. Thus it was that the first and simplest reading in *Webster's Spelling Book* began with, "No man may put off the law of God," and ended with the moral catechism, starting with the question, "Is pride commendable?" [1] Thus it was that the early school readers attempted to cover the field of morals and manners in an effort to stamp "lessons" indelibly on the mind of every pupil.

[1] C. Johnson, *The Country School* (N. Y., 1907), 10.

Even later school readers still clung to moral inculca-
tion as an educational ideal.[1] Take, for example, a
sampling of the contents of the 1837 edition of *McGuffey's
Fourth Reader*. There are three selections showing the
effect of intemperance upon home life; two selections
from Henry Ward Beecher showing the necessity of
education; another making a plea for common schools,
and two others on the value of mathematics; another
that portrays the "elevated character of women;"
two selections on the effects of gambling and on the
criminality of dueling; there are selections showing that
the righteous are never forsaken and that religion is
the only basis for society, and another asserting that
no other community of men on the globe has surpassed
the Pilgrim Fathers for moral worth; there are Milton's
picture of Satan and Death at the gate of Hell and,
near the end, Addison's *Vision of Mirza*, John's vision
of The Celestial City, Solomon's words about the wise
son and glad father, and Isaiah's vision of Zion redeemed.
So it is that the "record of American education is a long
story of idealism which has touched literature at every
turn. The red schoolhouse on the hill-top or at the
crossroads, the log-colleges in forgotten hamlets, the
universities founded by great states, are all a record of
the American faith—which has sometimes been called
a fetich—in education."[2]

Calvinistic individualism sought in America to build
a church without a bishop and a state without a king.
Since each soul was individually responsible to its God,
it must look to its own priming. Without education one
could not read and interpret the scriptures. Then, how

[1] H. H. Vail, *A History of the McGuffey Readers* (Cleveland,
1911), 6–7.

[2] Bliss Perry, *The American Mind* (Boston, 1912), 99.

could one be sure of his salvation? It is the educated individual that must save himself and the state.

Again, there is no surer evidence of this tendency to idealize education than is seen in the biographies and stories of struggling country boys who made by force their merits known. Many are the stories from Franklin to Lincoln of boys and mid-night oil or burning pine knots, struggling to realize this vague ideal called education. Franklin's Poor Richard affirmed, "The doors of Wisdom are never shut" and "God helps them that help themselves." There is no better example than Franklin himself, of living by the truth of these maxims. Though he had only about two years of "schooling," he was always a student and an omnivorous reader. He became the prototype of many an ambitious boy.[1] Time was in America when the country boy raised a calf, led him over the mountain to the nearest town to market, and remained for a term in the academy. The Schoolmaster in *Snowbound* fought his way unassisted. Locke Amsden went about his work of boiling maple syrup with his head full of figures and grammar puzzles.[2] The father of an eminent Princeton professor used to say when work became pressing on the farm: "Too much books! Too much books!" The young Brahmin in *Elsie Venner* left college to go to teaching because he did not have the money to finish, but kept a grim determination to see it through unaided.

Another phase of the idealization of education was that of regarding it as a means to power. The school was the practical form that the thoughts of the Puritans took in their quest for truth.[3] Just as transcendentalism

[1] Ford, *The Many-sided Franklin* (N. Y., 1899), 87–88.

[2] D. P. Thompson, *Locke Amsden*, 1847, 13.

[3] Channing, *United States* 1765–1865. Macmillan, 1896, 22–24. ATLANTIC MONTHLY, 128–355. Thompson, op. cit., 19.

took practical expression in the Brook Farm experiment, so in a larger way this zeal for education was focused in the school for the conservation of power. Jefferson, when thwarted in his first efforts to establish the University of Virginia, wrote pessimistically to Joseph W. Cabell: "All the states but our own are sensible that knowledge is power."[1] Channing says the colonists valued nearly everything in this way—money, position, education. To this end the Virginia planter employed private tutors for his son or sent him back to England to school. Even the clergy of the eighteenth century were not without this thirst for power.

If after the Revolution the enthusiasm for education was allowed to burn low, it was not long to remain in this state. Early in the century Harvard College was to be transformed from "little more than a boy's school" into an association of scholars, orators, and alert divines.[2] The new life began to flow into New England from abroad, especially from Germany. By 1839 Massachusetts was launched upon her career of teacher-training. Thereafter wherever emigrants from New England went, in the expansion of America, whether in Michigan, Ohio, or Indiana, schools began to spring up, and state legislatures began to copy the systems of Massachusetts and Connecticut. "Wherever the New Englander travels," wrote Lowell in 1865, "churches, schools, and colleges tell him where the men of his race have been, or their influence has penetrated."[3] To Lowell the little square, one-story schoolhouse was a kind of original fortification

---

[1] *The Chronicles of America* (New Haven, 1921), Vol. 33, 95.

[2] Wendell and Greenough, *History of Literature in America* (N. Y., 1904), 211.

[3] Works, *New England Two Centuries Ago* (Boston, 1910), Vol. II, 1.

invented by the founders of New England. "It was the great discovery of our Puritan forefathers," he asserts, "and by means of this discovery we have become a free and independent nation."[1]

That the older states of New England was a fountain head for education is echoed in American fiction. In Holland's novel, Arthur Bonnicastle's father at the insistence of the mother left the mountain farm in New Hampshire to come to Bradford where his children might receive a better education. Visitors came from Massachusetts to the Vermont, upstate home of Locke Amsden and later sent him books; this visit proved to be the turning point in his life.[2] The Hoosier School master was a torch-bearer into the "diggins" of Flat Creek. The frontier schoolmaster was, like Rostand's *Chanticleer*, a bringer of light into the world, into the dark and lonely valleys, behind the mountains, to the headwaters of the "Kingdom Come."[3]

[1] Ibid., 16–18.

[2] D. P. Thompson, *Locke Amsden* (Boston, 1847).

[3] ATLANTIC MONTHLY, May–December, 1922.

Lucy Furman, *Quare Women*.

John Fox Jr., *The Trail of the Lonesome Pine* (N. Y., 1905).

Thomas, *The Frontier Schoolmaster* (Montreal, 1881).

Alexander, *The Old Log Schoolhouse* (Philadelphia, 1864).

Caroline M. Kirkland, *A New Home—Who'll Follow or Glimpses of Western Life* (1839).

William Peter Strickland, *Pioneers of the West, or Life in the Woods*, (1855).

Anna Howard Shaw, *The Story of a Pioneer* (N. Y., 1905).

Even middle Georgia shows a New England influence. See Report of the Commissioner of Education in the United States 1896, 839–874.

Richard Malcolm Johnston, *Educational Life in Middle Georgia*.

All these show the schoolmaster as a light-bringer from civilization.

But as a matter of fact, the Scotch-Irish and Scotch who came to America in the latter part of the eighteenth and in the beginning of the nineteenth centuries were a sinewy race of men with conviction scarcely less strong than the Puritans. The great number of schools, academies and colleges established by these covenanters throughout the middle and south Atlantic and middle western states testify to their zeal for education—a zeal perhaps given too little credit in reckoning factors in American history, though no doubt their head-strong individualism as well as their religious convictions prevented them from entering wholeheartedly for a time into the idea of public education. To follow the ancestors of Woodrow Wilson, late comers to American shores, is to see the predominating desire to know as characteristic of this race.[1]

Very rarely in America have bitter thrusts been made at education, and these have been made in recent years. The old FARMER'S ALMANAC satirized the incompetent teacher, as did Irving, Daniel Pierce Thompson, Richard Malcom Johnston, and William Hawley Smith. Trumbull laughs at the "Progress of Dulness" in an effort to be witty; but the school as an institution has seldom been struck. The English idea, *that people can be educated above their station*, has been late in coming to America. Only since the recent advances in psychology, does it seem that the question of limiting educational opportunity has been raised. The number of Henry Adamses who have seen only futility in all education is not large.

On the other hand, the popularity of all grades of education attests the widespread tendency among the masses to surround it with romance. On the subway a

[1] Baker, *Life and Letters of Woodrow Wilson* (N. Y., 1927), 1–46, 73.

gum-chewing shop girl is busy with a college hero featured in the DAILY NEWS. Rotary clubs print the chorus of Gus Edward's "School Days" in their song books and sing of "Dear old golden rule days" of the nineties. In 1926 vaudeville stars sing "School Day Sweethearts" (Words and music by Glen Edwards)—she in heavy shoes, calico, with two long plaits of hair tied with blue ribbons and hanging down her back; he barefoot, with the inevitable patch on his overalls, bearing a slingshot in one hip pocket. At the movies crowds grow enthusiastic on seeing a young collegiate football star defeat a champion pugilist. This same star is presented as successfully having graduated from a school of engineering and as inventing a radio safety device for locomotives, which brings him fame and fortune. Thus has the college been popularized in America and crowds continue to urge entrance at her doors. The difference between this and the preceding generations in this regard is the difference in advertising media. In those days the expression of New England mothers, who, like Locke Amsden's mother, were always saying to their sons that their highest aspiration for them was that they should become educated, Christian men, has had a telling weight in American educational and literary history.

Today education in America is a business of gigantic proportions, but even business may have a firm foundation in its aspirations. The schools of America fulfill in part the dreams of what education should do for a people. If the elder races halt or end their lesson, America still takes up the task eternal, believing that the secret and science of power is in education. Dazzled somewhat by the glory of the present as she still faces westward, she aims at a still more glorious future with a school system that will be able to discover and stimulate inventors, statesmen, musicians, artists, and poets. The thought is prevalent that America is now ripe for artistic production.   At the beginning of the nineteenth century when Sydney Smith asked his taunting question about an American book, he added, "Others claim honor because of things done by a long line of ancestors; an American glories in the achievement of a distant posterity.   Others appeal to history; an American appeals to prophecy."   Not only has such a statement been justified in our national history, but it is essentially true as an American attitude at the present time.   We are still a "nation of idealists," affirms Mr. Irving Babbitt.[1]

If by idealization in education one may mean the construction in the imagination of certain values together with an adventurous spirit in moving toward those values, if one so means that education should be forward- and not backward-looking, that culture comes in the present and the future and not by imitating the past, then John Dewey, our latest educational philosopher, may be said to idealize democratic education.[2]   Like Emerson, though going much farther, he may be said to be a practical idealist in educational matters.   "Our public education is a potential means for effecting the transfiguration of modern life into sentiment and imagination," says Dewey.[3]   Though success in the adventure is not pre-destined, the enterprise, how to turn materialistic and industrial America into cultural America, is "one of heroic dimensions."   Certainly we shall not do it by "plaintive eulogies of past culture.   What is alive and compelling in our education moves toward some undis-covered future."

[1] THE FORUM MAGAZINE, February, 1928, 175.

[2] Woodridge Riley, *American Thought from Puritanism to Pragmatism* (N. Y., 1915), 289–318, 299–302.

[3] Culture and Education, NEW REPUBLIC, July, 1916.

CHAPTER III

EDUCATIONAL THEMES IN COLONIAL LITERATURE

One would scarcely think to look into the literature of the colonial period of America for the treatment of the schoolmaster and his school as a literary theme; yet when the journals, autobiographies, diaries, verse, and such other works of the seventeenth and eighteenth centuries as are listed in Mr. Whitcomb's *Chronological Outlines of American Literature* are examined, the school, it is seen, attracts considerable attention. Incidental though this attention may be, it is, nevertheless, of interest in this study as a background for the later treatment of the school as a literary theme. In general the early writers of America, being especially attracted by religious and political subjects, did not see many literary possibilities in the school. An occasional eulogy on the life and work of some schoolmaster or a journal record of a cruel pedagogue, an oration or essay urging educational reform, an occasional poem satirizing the pedantry of the time, with here and there scattered through the early school readers a glimpse of school life, is about all that may be found. Yet these few instances have been of sufficient literary interest to attract the notice of well-known anthologists of early American literature—M. C. Tyler, Duyckinck, Griswold, Stedman and Hutchinson, and Trent and Wells. Outside the pale of the anthologist the school frequently becomes the subject in travel literature of the period and the almanac-maker utilizes it as a subject of interest to farmers. Belles-lettres as such did not appear in America until the beginning of the nineteenth century and it is here that we get the first enduring picture of the schoolmaster and his school.

If the authors and writers of the colonial period were Englishmen living in America, the schoolmasters of New England were also Englishmen transplanting English educational systems and traditions and using for the most part English textbooks. The Puritans, to whom we owe most of our educational development and who left records of schoolmasters of interest, brought with them from England three types of schools—the dame school, the writing school, and the Latin Grammar school, all of which are mentioned in the literature of this early period. With the beginning of English emigration to America the wave of zeal for founding Latin Grammar schools reached its crest and this impulse was felt not only in New England, but in the central and southern colonies. Besides the famous Latin schools of Eton, St. Pauls, Westminster, Rugby, Harrow, Repton, Uppingham, and the Merchant Taylors' School, of which some had been founded as early as the fourteenth century, we are told that more schools were established under Queen Elizabeth's reign than at any other period in English history. In a *Description of England*[1] we read: "There are a great number of Grammar Schools throughout the realm, and those very liberally endowed, for the better relief of poor scholars, so that there are not many corporate towns now under the Queen's dominion that have not one grammar school at the least with a sufficient living for a master and usher appointed to the same."

[1] W. Harrison in *Holinshed*, 1587, BK II, Chapter 3, *prope finem.*

The grammar school of Shakespeare's day was primarily a school for learning Latin. The poet revealed his familiarity with Lily's *Latin Grammar* (1566, 1568, 1574) in a scene from *The Merry Wives of Windsor* (IV, 1) in which the Welsh parson and schoolmaster, Sir Hugh Evans, asks the boy William "some questions in his accidence." The words *lapis*, and *pulcher* referred to in this quiz as well as the statement that "articles are borrowed of the pronouns," are found on the first two pages of the Grammar. Many of the poet's Latin words and phrases can also be traced to this book.[1] His use of Aesop's *Fables*, seven of which are fairly distinctly referred to, may be due to his study of them in the Latin versions used in the grammar school.[2]

The discipline of Shakespeare's day was vigorous. But whether Shakespeare actually had unpleasant experiences at school we do not know. The two schoolmasters that he characterized, Holofernes of *Love's Labor's Lost* and the Welsh schoolmaster, Evans, of *The Merry Wives of Windsor*, are mild and genial and represent the better rural type of the time. Pinch, however, of the *Comedy of Errors* is satirized as a "hungry lean-faced villian, a mere anatomy, a mountebank, a threadbare juggler, a fortune-teller, a needy hollow-eyed, sharp-looking wretch, a living dead man." This cruelty had been the subject of an after-dinner speech in London when, in 1563, Roger Ascham, then the Latin Secretary to Queen Elizabeth, was dining with Sir William Cecil (afterwards Lord Burleigh). Ascham argued that it was wrong "to beat nature in a child for a fault" stating, too, that "scholars are commonly beat for the making of Latin when the master were more worthy to be beat

---

[1] *Shakespeare's England* (Oxford, 1927), 232.

[2] "The Fox and the Grapes" in *All's Well*, II, 1, 73.

for the mending or rather the marring of the same; the master many times being as ignorant as the child of what to say properly and fitly. For commonly many schoolmasters—be of so crooked a nature, as, when they meet with a hard-witted scholar, they rather break him than bow him, rather mar him than mend him. For when the schoolmaster is angry with some other matter, then will he soonest fall to beat his scholars." It is not strange therefore that the first note struck with regard to the school in American literature is one of cruelty—the cruelty of the schoolmaster.

Whatever the occasion for the beating was, John Winthrop records in his *Journal* April 4, 1639, how one Nathaniel Eaton,[1] a Puritan schoolmaster and the first president of Harvard, who, upon falling out with his usher, Nathaniel Briscoe, a boy of gentle birth, fell upon him with a walnut cudgel a yard long and "big enough to kill a horse" and beat him for two hours with two hundred blows about the head and shoulders. The boy, who by this time thought he would be murdered, began to pray, and Eaton beat him all the more for "taking the name of God in vain." Not satisfied with this he took his complaint against the boy to the magistrates who, to Eaton's surprise, insisted on hearing the boy's story. Eaton was brought to trial in open court and it was found that he had a habit of beating a student until "he had subdued the party to his will." Complaint was also made against the ill and scant diet; for while the students paid a large allowance for their board, their diet was ordinarily "nothing but porridge and pudding, and that

[1] John Winthrop, *Journal* (Hartford, 1790), 184–188. A Journal of the transactions and occurrences in the settlement of Massachusetts and other New England colonies from the year 1630 to 1644.

very homely." But the schoolmaster put this "off to his wife."

The trial went on for days, Eaton all the while "justifying himself." It was finally decided that because of the scandal to religion and the offense which would be given to such as might intend their children thither, he should pay the usher twenty pounds and be debarred the teaching of children within the jurisdiction of the court. Eaton, however, upon finding out that the church at Cambridge was to try him also, fled the country, leaving his wife and children behind together with a debt of one thousand pounds and bills charged to his brother's agent in England. He took ship for Virginia where, Winthrop in 1640 records, he took upon him to be a minister but was given up of God to extreme pride and sensuality, "being usually drunken, as the custom is there." He sent for his wife and children. "Her friends here persuaded her to stay a while, but she went notwithstanding, and the vessel was never heard of after." No doubt this was one of the Providences of God in the destruction of the wicked along with the incident of the mouse that gnawed the prayer book or the children that providentially escaped the falling logs.

To Winthrop, also, it seemed unavoidable for an immigrant to Virginia to become a victim of pride, sensuality and drunkenness. But as for the case of Eaton versus the usher, he records for us a chapter in the history of the rod, a chapter destined to be torn from the page of education in America. The education which had as its chief aim the subduing of one will to the will of another was soon to become offensive, especially to the gentle born. The school must succeed in America, and it could not succeed if parents refused to send their children to such a master. Moreover such punishment was in truth a scandal to religion; instead of idealizing, it degraded education.

The life of the usher in the grammar school of the time, if we are to believe this account and others of him in England, must have been one of great drudgery. John Brinsley in *The Stommer School* (1612) tells how the school should begin at six and how at nine the students were to be given an intermission of fifteen minutes "for honest recreation, for breakfast or to prepare their exercises against the master's coming." This early work of opening the school was often left to the usher. Robert Lloyd, (1733–1764), who later became an usher to his father at the Westminster school, wrote of the intolerable drudgery of the school usher, saying that if he were empowered to wreak his vengeance on his foe he would make him usher in a school; for there one spends his time working on a barren soil,

> And laboring with incessant pains
> To cultivate a blockhead's brains—
> Still to be pinioned down to teach
> The syntax and the parts of speech;
> Or perhaps what is drudgery worse,
> The links and points and rules of verse—
> And while a paltry stipend earning
> He sows the richest seeds of learning—
> No joys! alas! his toils beguile,
> His own is fallow all the while,—
> He turns like horses in a mill,
> Nor getting on nor standing still;
> For little way his learning reaches,
> Who reads no more than what he teaches.

This disgust with the school is later echoed in the poetry of John Trumbull and others of the Hartford Wits. Even of late years Henry Adams expressed revulsion in trying to thrust learning on "unwilling minds," a phrase closely akin to "blockhead brains" which both Lloyd and Trumbull used.

But if schoolmasters were cruel, their scholars were not all saintly. On April 5, 1644,[1] Winthrop records that "two of our ministers sons being students in the college robbed two dwelling houses in the night, of some fifteen pounds—being found out they were ordered by Governors of the college to be there whipped, which was performed by the President himself; yet they were about twenty years of age—and after this they were brought into the court and ordered to make two-fold satisfaction or to serve so long for it. We had yet no particular punishment for burglary." Again at the first commencement, 1642,[2] complaint was made to the governors of "two young men of good quality lately come out of England, for foul misbehavior, in swearing and ribaldry speeches, for which, though they were adult they were corrected in the college, and sequestered for a time." "Corrected" had a stronger meaning than at present, and "sequestered" was not used in the poetic sense.

The spirit of the times is also shown in the by-laws of Harvard College and the Grammar School with the fines attached:

> neglecting to repeat the sermon, 9d;
> entertaining persons of ill character, not exceeding 1s, 6d;
> profane cursing, not exceeding 2s, 6d;
> graduates playing cards, not exceeding 5s;
> undergraduates playing cards, not exceeding, 1s, 6d;
> lying, not exceeding, 5s;
> drunkenness, not exceeding 1s, 6d;
> refusing to give evidence, 3s;
> sending freshmen in study time, 9d.[3]

---

[1] Ibid., 333.
[2] Ibid., 265.
[3] Mary Crawford, *Social Life in Old New England*, Chapter II, 61.

Even as late as 1772 Phillip Vickers Fithian shows that the life at Princeton then and that at Harvard in 1642 were much the same—the curriculum, the daily program, the rules and precepts, the attached grammar schools under the direction of the presidents, and the requirements for degrees.[1] Fithian records cases of expulsion not for the usual drunkenness, swearing, following street women on Nassau, or Sabbath-breaking, but "they were sent from this Seminary—for stealing hens."[2] He declares that turkey-stealing was as common a practice among the boys as revivals of religion were among the authorities. At this time Princeton had over a hundred students with more than a fourth of them belonging to the Grammar School, which had been established during the administration of President Burr.[3] Fithian nonchalantly remarks in a letter to his friend that "we have had a considerable stir of religion in college since you went away; Lewis Willison is thought to have got religion, and the formerly abandoned Glover is seeking the way to heaven."[2]

No doubt the coarse fare of the students was provocative of some misdemeanors, for it is mentioned three times in Winthrop's Journal, once in the case of Eaton and twice when the elders[4] dined at the college common, where they had their diet after the manner of the scholars "but somewhat better," and where at the first commencement they "ate with the scholars for the purpose of encouragement."

[1] *New England's First Fruits*, Roger Williams, London, 1643.
Massachusetts Historical Collection, 1792, Vol. I, 242–246.

[2] Philip Vicker's Fithian, *Journal and Letters*, Student at Princeton College, 1770–1772; Princeton Historical Association, Princeton, 1900, 22–30.

[3] McClean, *History of College of New Jersey*, 259, 266, 268.

[4] Winthrop, op. cit. (July 4, 1643), 307.

But not all the English schoolmasters in America are represented as Nathaniel Eatons. If Winthrop is the truest representative of colonial life, his temperament is essentially judicial.[1] While he tells of the legal transactions which established free schools at Roxbury, he leaves to Cotton Mather the narration of the zeal of mild-spirited John Eliot whose endeavors there resulted in more scholars than in "any town of its bigness, or, if I mistake not, of twice its bigness in all New England."[2] It is Cotton Mather also who eulogizes the work of two of the more famous colonial schoolmasters: Elijah Corlett (1611–1687) for forty-three years head of the Cambridge Latin School, and Ezekiel Cheever (1614–1708) who was for thirty-eight years head of the Boston Latin School. These, as many of the teachers in the early grammar schools, were graduates of Oxford or Cambridge and were noted for their kindness as well as firmness in their treatment of slow pupils. Both were celebrated in the well-known couplet:

> 'Tis Corlett's pains and Cheever's, we must own, .
> That thou, New England, art not Scythia Grown.

The work of Cheever persists almost as a tradition in America. Articles on him have appeared repeatedly in the magazines, the latest life of "the first schoolmaster of Boston" being published in 1912. Hawthorne in paying tribute to him avers: "Almost all the great men of that period, and for many years back had been whipped into eminence" through his "fatherly tenderness."[3] Michael Wigglesworth of *The Day of Doom* fame went to school to him in New Haven and "got forward apace;" President Stiles of Yale College said in his Diary that

[1] Tyler, *American Literature* (N. Y., 1878), Vol. I, 132.

[2] Mather, *Magnalia*, Vol. I, 551, 1855.

[3] Hawthorne, *Grandfather's Chair* (Boston, 1898), 86.

Cheever wore a long, white beard terminating in a point and that "when he stroked it to the point, it was a sign for the boys to clear out;" and John Barnard (1681–1770) tells a lively incident in his autobiography[1] of how the master, to whom he had been sent in his eighth year, said to him one day: "You Barnard, I know you can do well enough if you will; but you are so full of play that you hinder your classmates from getting their lessons; and therefore if any of them cannot perform their duty I shall correct you for it." It turned out that one of the boys knowing this, willfully neglected his duty, so that Barnard was corrected "for several days." Growing tired of this persecution the lad took the matter in hand himself and gave his classmate such a hearty drubbing that he "never came to school anymore."

But it was perhaps in Cheever's last illness and death that he was best remembered in literary way. His former pupil, Samuel Sewall, in the ninety-fourth year of his master's life notes in his Diary, August 12, 1708: "Mr. Cheever is abroad and hears Mr. Cotton Mather preach. This was the last of his going abroad. Was taken very sick, and like to die of a Flux." The diary keeps in touch with the old man until August 21, when we read: "Mr. Oakes tells me Mr. Cheever died last night. He has labored in that calling (teaching) skillfully, diligently, constantly, religiously seventy years. A rare instance of Piety, Health, Strength, Serviceableness. The Welfare of the Province was much upon his spirit. He abominated Perriwigs." Cotton Mather, another pupil, preached the funeral, concluding with an elegy:[2]

[1] *Massachusetts History: Sociology*—Third Series, Vol. V.   See also Trent, *Revolutionary Literature*, Vol. III, 261–265.

[2] Rev. Cotton Mather, D. D., *Corderius Americanus, A Discourse on the Good Education of Children* (Boston, 1708).

Almighty tribe of well-instructed youth,
Tell what they owe to him, and tell the truth.

Benjamin Thompson, the renowned poet of New England, whose tombstone at Roxbury tells us he was a learned schoolmaster and physician and the first native-born American poet (1644–1714), also published a broadside at Cheever's death:[1]

Eight parts of speech this day wear mourning gowns,
Declin'd Verbs, Pronouns, Participles, and Nouns.
And not declined, Adverbs and Conjunctions,
In Lillie's Porch they stand to do their functions
With Preposition; but most affection
Was still observed in the interjection.

Like Charles Lamb's old schoolmaster, Cheever believed all learning was contained in the languages, and like Browning's Grammarian parts of speech were ripe when the death rattle was in the throat. Unlike Lamb's old master he seemed at home in the society of others, though he lived like Gulliver among his little people. Nathaniel Ames wrote in his Almanac of his death:[2] "He left off at last without being tired, but simply because he was obliged to."

And well might the parts of speech put on mourning at his death, for the old Latin Grammar School was destined to die, or to be displaced by the more American academy. However, Lilly's *Latin Grammar*, with which Shakespeare had been familiar, is the same as that upon whose husks Tom Brainless dieted in Trumbull's *Progress of Dulness*, an edition of which appeared as late as 1817. Cheever's *Accidence* went through seventeen editions

[1] NOTE: Reproduced by Dr. Samuel A. Green in his Ten Facsimile Reproductions (Boston, 1902), III. See also Earle, *Child Life in Colonial Days*, Opposite 134.

[2] Edited with notes by Samuel Briggs, Cleveland, 1891, 19.

before the Revolution, the eighteenth having been printed in Boston, 1785 and the last in 1838.[1] This study of Latin persisted far into the nineteenth century in New England, for E. E. Hale in his *New England Boyhood* tells of boys, "bright fellows who went off early into business because they would not go through the slavery of learning Latin Grammar."

In England Crabbe wrote (1810) of Borough lads who

"O'er a grammar waste their sprightly powers."

Bacon had preached the necessity of altering the whole system of knowing in order to get away from bookmakers; and Milton urged the bringing of the curriculum into closer touch with life; while Locke[2] planned a practical course of study for sons who were to be leaders. Hugh Jones complains in his *Present State of Virginia* (1724) that lads sent back to England are kept drudging "on in what is of little use to them, in pedantic methods, too tedious for their volatile genius," and are "imprisoned and enslaved to what they hate and think useless." Pope and Swift struck bitterly at pedagogical methods with their disciplinary ideals and general neglect of the English tongue. Gulliver, visiting Lagado, the capital of the floating island, found at the academy students and teachers alike employed in futile studies while the country lay miserably waste, while houses lay in ruin, and while crowds of people swarmed the city streets with gaunt faces. He soon saw that nothing in this country could invite him to stay since he learned that not a town of any consequence in the kingdom was without such an academy. Pope more bitterly satirizes educational practices.

[1] THE BAY STATE MONTHLY, Vol. I, 99.
[2] John Locke, *Some Thoughts Concerning Education* (London, 1693).

In the *Dunciad* (1742, Bk. IV) the goddess Dullness comes in majesty to destroy science and order and to inaugurate the reign of Dunces. A birch-crowned specter, the representative of schoolmasters, rose, his brow dripping with infants' blood, and assures the goddess that the chief aim of schools is to keep youths out of the way of real knowledge by confining them to words. Thus through the aid of the schools Chaos is restored to her throne and darkness settles down upon the world.[1]

With the emigration of the English scholar and recluse, Francis Knapp, to America near the beginning of the eighteenth century, Pope began his reign in the colonies, as the "sacred bard" who proclaimed his "shining page to our dark world."[2] Satire became the order of the day, and the school and educational methods were frequently the butt of ridicule. Moreover, by the time Popian satire had reached America the battle against the classics of the old Latin school had already begun, and before the end of the century the academy had become firmly established. In his *Autobiography* for the year 1743, Franklin notes that he had every reason to be satisfied with being a citizen of Philadelphia except for the fact that there was no provision for defense "nor *for a complete education of the youth.*"[3] He, therefore, was soon to propose and to establish a Philosophical Society (1744) which was to receive from its members papers outlining

---

[1] As late as 1876 Samuel Butler, with irony as mordant and wit as caustic as Pope's, exposes the work of a mid-century schoolmaster in a well-known public school of England. See Samuel Butler, *The Way of All Flesh*, Chapter XXVI–XL (N. Y., 1925).

[2] Duyckinck, op. cit., Vol. I, 72.

[3] *Autobiography*, edited by H. A. Davidson (N. Y., 1908), 178, 189–191.

courses of study whose bearing upon the trend of the curriculum in the young republic was to be significant.[1] In his own pamphlet, *Proposals Relating to the Education of Youth in Pennsylvania* (1749), he took special pains[2] to provide for the study of English and other practical subjects. Though he advocated the study of Latin and Greek for those who "intended to become ministers or lawyers," he asserts that for other students time spent on them "might be better employed in education for such a country as ours."

Francis Hopkinson (1737–1791) who was the first student enrolled in the new academy (1751) and the first to receive a diploma for a degree in the college of Philadelphia (1757)[3] wrote a poem, "*Science*," (1762) in which he compliments his college and praises in detail its liberal curriculum.[4] Later, after the college had returned to the control of the Latinists, Hopkinson bitterly denounced the *Learned Languages* and the excessive pedantry of grammarians.[5] It was at this time that Franklin near the end of his life wrote his *Observations Relating to the Intentions of the Original Founders of the*

---

[1] See Hansen, A. O., *Liberalism and American Education in the Eighteenth Century* (N. Y., 1926), Chapter IV, for a full discussion of the educational work of this society. Also The Bureau of Education, Circular No. 2, Benjamin Franklin and the University of Pennsylvania, Washington, 1892, 40–75.

[2] Smyth, *The Life and Writings of Benjamin Franklin* (N. Y., 1906), Vol. II, 386–396.

[3] George Everett Hastings, *The Life and Works of Francis Hopkinson* (Chicago, 1927), 43–45.

[4] Hastings, op. cit., 45–49.

[5] Hopkinson, *Miscellaneous Essays*, Vol. II. "On the Learned Education," 1–12.

"On the Learned Languages," 41–48.

"A Reply to the Foregoing Speech," 49–57.

Academy in Philadelphia (June, 1789).[1] "It will appear," he asserts, "how much the English learning was insisted upon in it [the original proposal] and I have good reason to know that this was a prevailing part of the motives for subscribing with most of the benefactors."[2] "Notwithstanding this good resolution of the trustees, it seemed the execution of it was neglected. The Latinists were combined to decry the English School as useless—"It is without example," they said, "that a school for teaching the vulgar tongue and the sciences in that tongue was ever joined with a college."[3]

As early as 1722 Franklin had announced his attitude toward the classics.[4] But sixty-two years later in his *Remarks Concerning the Savages of North America*, he gives us one of his most effective bits of satire in showing the differences between the learning that comes from grammars and books and that which comes from life.[5] When it is proposed to the Indians of the Six Nations that a fund is available for the education of a half dozen of their sons at William and Mary, Franklin humorously has the Indians make a counter proposal that the white men send a dozen of their sons to them. "We know," say the Indians, "you highly esteem the kind of learning taught in those colleges—but several of our young people were formerly brought up at colleges in the North Provinces—and when they came back they were bad runners, ignorant of the means of living in the woods,

[1] *The Life and Writings of Benjamin Franklin*, op. cit., Vol. X, 9–31.

Bureau of Education, op, cit., 39–51.

[2] Bureau of Education, op. cit., 40.

[3] Ibid., 46.

[4] Carl Van Doren, *Franklin and Edwards* (N. Y., 1920), "Do Good Papers," No. IV, 1–4.

[5] Ibid., 176–182.

unable to bear either cold or hunger—and spoke our language imperfectly."

Four years later Freneau published *The Indian Student or The Force of Nature* (1788),[1] which showed the deadening effect of the atmosphere of Harvard upon a young barbarian. Here men talk heathen Greek or gabble Hebrew lore to their student. For a while he learns their rules of grammar, but soon the hours grow tedious in the heavy-moulded lecture room and he "sighs to be a-hunting in the woods" and "to see the setting sun." Here "no mystic wonder fires his mind." Musty books of Latin could not take the place of the silver lakes and the streams of his boyhood. So he leaves the college halls to return to "nature's ancient forests." Freneau, though somewhat idealizing Indian life, undoubted meant to express his reaction against the classics along with his contemporaries. A few years earlier in a poem called "The Silent Academy" (1781) he had treated romantically,[2] all the bygone life of the academy he had attended but in his "Epistle to a Student of Dead Languages" he has the same hostile feeling as expressed in the Indian poem against the study of Latin and Greek:

> I pity him, who, at no small expense,
> Has studied sound instead of sense;
> He, proud some antique gibberish to attain;
> Of Hebrew, Greek or Latin, Vain,
> Devours the husk, and leaves the grain.
> In his own language Homer writ and read,
> Nor spent his life on poring on the dead:
> Why then your native language not pursue
> In which all ancient sense (that's worth review)
> Glows in translation fresh and new?[3]

[1] Fred A. Pattee, *Poems of Philip Freneau, Poet of the American Revolution*, Princeton (1907), Vol. II, 371, 372.

[2] Ibid., Vol. I, 182, 183.

[3] Ibid., Vol. III, 121.

A contemporary of Hopkinson and Freneau and a leader in the production of satiric verse in imitation of Pope was John Trumbull (1756–1841), perhaps the most popular of the Hartford Wits. Born at Lebanon, Connecticut, he tells us he went to school there to Nathan Tisdale, who for thirty years was distinguished for keeping one of the best schools in New England. In 1772, when the master had a stroke of paralysis, Trumbull, who was then just out of Yale, taught the school until the master's recovery in the spring. He had seventy or eighty pupils ranging from those "just lisping the A B C to young men preparing for college," some of whom were his seniors. By August he had finished the first part of his long satiric poem on provincial ignorance and the insane curriculum of the time. In his preface[1] he asserts that except for one neighboring province "ignorance wanders unmolested" in the colleges, that students may graduate unchallenged after four years of dozing, and that the ancient languages are of little value in any business or profession in life. He says that he was prompted to write the poem by the hope that "it might be of use to point out in a clear, concise and striking manner the general errors that hinder the advantages of education and the growth of piety."

The first part relates the adventures of Brainless Tom whose parents sent him to college to avoid the hard work they have known in trying to wrest a living from the stubborn soil of New England.

> Our Tom has grown a sturdy boy
> His progress fills my heart with joy;
> A steady soul that yields to rule,
> And quite ingenious too at school.

[1] *The Poetical Works of John Trumbull, II* (Hartford, 1820), printed by Samuel S. Goodrich.

> Our master says, (I'm sure he's right)
> There's not a lad in town so bright.
> He'll cypher bravely, write and read,
> And say his catechism and creed,
> And scorns to hesitate or falter
> In Primer, Spelling-book or Psalter.
> Hard Work indeed he does not love it;
> His Genius is too much above it.
> Give him a good substantial teacher
> I'll lay he'll make a special preacher.
> I've loved good learning all my life;
> We'll send the lad to college, wife.

In preparation for college the youth is sent to the village parson where he spends two years feeding "on the husks of Lily," murdering the verses of Virgil, and construing Tully into farce. Somehow, "no matter how," he gets into college and no sooner there than the college evil seizes on him—idleness.   It

> Stirs up seeds of dire disease
> Greek spoils his eyes, the print's so fine
> Grown dim with study or with wine.

Kind Headache, the Friend of Idleness, comes to set the blunderer free from his tasks.   But, according to the satirist, the studious boys are little better off; for despising English grammar, and "every nicer art that aids the tongue," they

> Read ancient authors o'er in vain
> Nor taste one beauty they contain
> And plodding on in one dull tone,
> Gain ancient tongues and lose their own.

The poet here expresses a hope that he may live to see the day when quackeries of learning will be exploded, when sense will preside over methods in education so that useful learning will spread over the land.   Returning to his hero who has now finished his four years of dozing and "taken in form his first degree," the poet brings him home with his head as empty as his purse. Since he is prepared to do nothing else, his father advises him to take a school. We next see him enthroned in the elbow chair of the village school, where

> He tries, with ease and unconcern
> To teach what ne'er himself could learn.

"His ragged regiment" gathered round him are taught "not to read, but fear and tremble;" for he

> Holds all good learning must depend
> Upon his rod's extremest end
> Whose great electric virtue's such,
> Each genius brightens at the touch;
> With threats and blows, incitements pressing
> Drives on his lads to learn each lesson;
> Thinks flogging cures all moral ills,
> And breaks their heads to break their wills.

The year ended, Tom decides to find what he thinks is easier employment—the ministry. The children rejoice at his going, but the parents grieve

> And seek again, their school to keep
> One just as good and just as cheap.

In spirit Tom belongs to the school of Ichabod Crane, except that, perhaps, Ichabod had no thought of changing his profession. What Ichabod might have been had he turned preacher may be seen in the lines which describe the result of Tom Brainless' training when he finally settles down in a community that knows no more than he does:

> He culls his text, and tills his farm,
> Does little good, and little harm;
> On Sunday, in his best array
> Deals forth the dullness of the day,
> And while above he spreads his breath,
> The yawning audience nod beneath.

The second part introduces to us Dick Hairbrain, a town fop, ridiculous in dress and empty of knowledge. It shows the folly of attempting to educate a natural fool. His father, the wealthiest farmer in the town, sent him to college to mend his brains; but in short his brain would not be mended; for when he tries to solve Newton's system, he finds his "wits in dark eclipse." The counterpart of Dick is Miss Harriet Simper who makes her appearance in the third part and illustrates the stupidity of fashionable education which attempted to produce coquettes.[1] At school her education "was none or worse than none," at home she

> Wastes long months in still more tawdry
> And useless labours of embroid'ry.

Sent to the city where ladies grow ecstatic over Pamela and gentlemen swear by Lovelace or spout the philosophy of Tristram Shandy, she takes her little town by storm when she returns, and dozens of admirers are victims of her jilting. At last she falls a victim to Dick Hairbrain who is as great a flirt as she. Dick, however, rejects her and she is discarded generally by the beaux. As a last resort she is compelled to accept Tom Brainless as the only fitting match to her own ill training and emptiness.

This poem constitutes the most important literary sidelight on education in America up to 1800. Not only did it announce the arrival of a new star in the literary heavens, but it foretold changes that were to take place in education when schools and colleges would expand their curricula, schoolmasters would cease to consider flogging as all important, and when women would be admitted capable of collegiate education. In an address

[1] NOTE: Timothy Dwight and others in their travels speak of the emptiness of female education in New England. See pp. 52-58.

at the Yale commencement September 12, 1770 on "The Use and Advantages of the Fine Arts," the youthful Trumbull predicted the time when the American poets would vie with Milton, Pope, Thomson, and Young, and when American prose would equal in charm that of Steele and Addison. Graduating, himself, in the school of Pope, he yet lacks Pope's finesse. Such rhymes as "pressing" and "lesson" Pope could not have tolerated, but Trumbull has couplets which rival the best in the age of Queen Anne, and these together with the increasing satire upon pedantry could not but have had weight upon the trend of education.

On the other hand Timothy Dwight, another of the Yale group of poets, sentimentalizes over the lot of schoolmasters in a long descriptive poem "Greenfield Hill" (N. Y., 1794) which, in its imitation of Goldsmith, presents a picture of a New England academy and of the inferior school. Writing the verses merely to amuse himself, "to gain a temporary relief from the pressure of melancholy," he, nevertheless, succeeded as well as his material would allow in delineating not only Greenfield, but the inland towns of New England generally.

As in Goldsmith, Dwight presents the church and the school as twin lanterns of the law, the parson and the schoolmaster being presented side by side. Spelling-books often displayed cuts showing this intimate relation between the church and the school, the school always raising a somewhat humbler spire to the skies. Not only in this poem but in his *New England Travels*, Dwight observes that the "multitude of schools everywhere" go "parallel with ministers and churches." The village preacher was always present at the final school examinations and exhibitions and was called upon for remarks in behalf of piety and education. On passing a schoolhouse in Boston one day and observing that it was being torn down so that the adjoining church could be enlarged, Joseph Green, (1706–1780) one of the most popular poets of his time composed the following humorous epigram:

> "A fig for learning, I tell you the town
>   To make the church larger, must pull the school down."
> "Unluckily spoken," replied Master Birch;
> "Then learning, I fear, stops the growth of the church."[1]

Trumbull, too, satirizes the church as the overseer of education.[2]   But if ministers were often teachers of the young,[3] schoolmasters were in turn required to "catechise their scholars in the principles of the Christian Religion—and to commend them unto God by prayer morning and evening, taking care that the scholars do reverently attend during the same."

Unlike Goldsmith's schoolmaster, Dwight's ruled without a rod as no doubt many good schoolmasters of New England did.[4]

> He knew little, but much he wished to know.
> Yet oft his students at his wisdom star'd,
> For many a student to his side repaired,
> Surprised, they heard him Dilworth's knots untie.
> And tell what lands beyond the Atlantic lie.
> Many his faults; his virtue's small and few;
> Some little good he did, or strove to do.

[1] Quoted in Kettle, Samuel, *Specimens of American Poetry* (Boston, 1829), Vol. I, 139.

[2] Tom Brainless got his preparation (in Latin) for college from a rural parson who had run the usual dull course of progress and had long since forgot all he knew of tongues.

[3] See Mather's account of John Cotton and John Eliot, *Magnalia* (Hartford, 1855), 252–286, 526–584.

[4] Pleasures of a Schoolmaster," NEW ENGLAND MAGAZINE, July, 1831, gives an excellent account of a kindhearted master who never whipped.

Children loved Dwight's schoolmaster; they feared Goldsmith's and "counterfeited glee" at his jokes. Goldsmith's master has no names of textbooks opprobriously attached to him as millstones about his neck, nor does he teach long sermons of morality by terrifying pictures of the *House of Sloth* such as Dwight portrayed. His portrait is more vividly real and more sharply focussed.

Perhaps the truest and most vivid picture of the colonial schoolmaster which has come down to us is that found in the novel *Margaret* by Sylvester Judd, (1845), a man whose genealogical and historical researches into prerevolutionary times aided him in writing what Lowell called "the most emphatically American book ever written."[1] In spite of Lowell's remarks Judd's schoolmaster was as typically English as he was colonial. The dress he wore—the three-cornered hat, the coat descending in long, square skirts to the calves of his legs, the white silk stockings, the paste knee and shoe buckles, the sleeves and shirts garnished with rows of silver buttons, the ruffle cuffs, the wig falling in rows over his shoulders, the tortoise-shell spectacles and gold-headed cane—all stamped him as a better class English schoolmaster of the eighteenth century.

The village in which he lived and taught, with its high-pitched roofs and jutting upper stories, its green, its five distilleries, its meeting-house with tall, slim spire and open belfry, its pillory, its pair of stocks and whipping post, had about it the atmosphere of Cobbett's rural England. Exempt from military service by his profession, the master had always been rated a Tory. He was a gentleman inveterately attached to the olden time. In his room were many mementos of the Kings of England,

[1] NORTH AMERICAN REVIEW, XIX, 209.

including an escutcheon bearing the head of King George. Once during the Revolution he was made prisoner for his symphathies with the mother country, and it was only by apologizing to the selectmen of the town that he was released.

His library as well as his prejudice toward English-made textbooks shows unquestionably his inclination. With the exception of a few contemporary American poets, his library was made up entirely of English writings—the works of Bolingbroke, Sterne, and Swift, the SPECTATOR and the RAMBLER together with the principal English poets, Burton's *Anatomy of Melancholy*, and *Peregrine Pickle*. *The New Spelling Book* of Daniel Fleming, late schoolmaster of the Bures in Suffolk, England, had long been his favorite speller, and it was with much ceremony that he presented it to his favorite pupil, Margaret.

True to the homeland, he loved his glass and "drank constantly and at times excessively." His religion, too, was that of Dr. Johnson, for when his pupil asked him what God was, he replied that girls should go quietly about their work and refrain from all such questions. His love of flogging also placed him in the Johnsonian tradition, for he believed the Swabian master who had administered 911,000 canings was the best. As for himself, he could never exceed "ten castigations per diem."

Goodrich's Master Stebbins of the "Uptown" school in Ridgefield was a schoolmaster much like Judd's. He taught in a little wooden building (20 × 30) covered with brown clapboards. In 1803, when Goodrich first went to him, this "model schoolmaster" of colonial days had been in charge for many years. He was a man about fifty, with a conciliating stoop in his shoulders, a long body, short legs, and a swaying walk. His hair, being thin and silvery, always fell in well-combed rolls over his coat collar. "His eye was blue and his dress invariably of the same color. Breeches and knee-buckles, blue-mixed stockings, and shoes with bright buckles, seemed as much a part of the man as his head and shoulders. On the whole his appearance was that of a middle class gentleman of the olden time, and he was in fact what he seemed."[1]

Besides the Latin Grammar school, which was the foundation on which the American Academy was built, the dame school was another English institution transplanted to America. Though it was widely popular in New England towns and villages in the eighteenth century, it failed to find any notable literary expression there, while in Great Britain such poets as Shenstone, Crabbe, and Henry Kirk White graced this humble theme with idyllic sanctity.

After the dame school became established in the district parishes as a summer primary school of colonial New England, various authors wrote of it entertainingly down to the middle of the nineteenth century. Dwight, in the frankly imitative poem, "Greenfield Hill," sentimentalizes over the dame school:

> Behold yon humbler mansion lifts its head
> Where infant minds to science door are led.
> As now, by kind indulgence loos'd to play,
> From place to place, from sport to sport they stray,
> How light their gambols frolic o'er the green!
> How their shrill voices cheer the rural scene!
> *Sweet harmless elves!* in Freedom's household born,
> *Enjoy the raptures of your transient morn.*

The Reverend John Barnard, minister in Marblehead, Massachusetts, (1681–1770) describes in his autobiog-

[1] Goodrich, *Recollections of a Life Time* (N. Y., 1856), 138–147.

raphy the dame school which he was attending in Boston, and reflects the beginnings of the monitorial system when he tells how he, at the age of six, "was appointed a sort of an usher to teach some children that were older than he as well as some smaller ones." Chief among those who have remembered the schoolmistress of the summer school are S. G. Goodrich (1793–1860) and Reverend Warren Burton (1800–1866).[1] What Goodrich has to say of this school has been often quoted as history: "It was the custom at this place (Ridgefield, Connecticut) to have a woman school in the summer months which was attended only by small children." Aunt Delight, the teacher, sat on a low chair and calling the pupils before her, would require each "to make his manners, consisting of a small nod, or jerk of the head." She would then place a Dilworth spelling book before the pupil, and pointing to the letters of the alphabet with a pointed buck-handled penknife, say:

"What's that?"

"A," was the response of the child.

"Stha-at?"

"B."

"Sna-at?"

"C."

"Sna-a-at?"

"D," etc.   Thus continues the monotonous process.[2]

[1] Goodrich, *Recollections of a Life Time* (N. Y., 1857), 34–38.

Burton, *The District School as It Was* (1833) (N. Y., 1897), 6–11, 20–24.

Even in 1926 Miss Hewins writing of "A Mid-century Child and Her Books" lovingly recalls a sunny room in an old-fashioned house where an old lady known as Aunt Electra was kindness itself to the children (17), who took their first steps in learning from her.

[2] Goodrich, op. cit., 36.

The schoolmistress in the dame schools of America is usually remembered in fiction as mild in discipline and as taking a keen interest in the welfare of her little charges.[1] Such is the picture of the dame in perhaps the most literary treatment of this school on this side the Atlantic—"The Schools of Olden Times."[2] While in this poem we catch a glimpse of little boys trudging to school on stick horses, the emphasis in these anonymous lines is upon the schoolmistress and the respect of the children for her. She did not, as Shenstone's schoolmistress, "boast unruly brats to tame." She is kind and quiet, teaching little boys to make their bow, to "put handles on the names" of elders in addressing them, and little girls to curtsy full low and "to hide her ankles 'neath her gown." She had no need of a bell with which to call her charge to books; only a rap on the pane was sufficient. Her dress of modest green calash or a calico Van Dyke "hung gracefully all round," and she never "sported pantlets, nor wore a bustle." She was as conservative and methodical as the dame of Shenstone's lively poem:

> With modest mein and lovely heart
> Her daily tasks were done,
> And, true as needle to the pole,
> The next one was begun.
>
> The days were all alike to her,
> The evenings just the same,
> And neither brought a change to us
> Till Saturday forenoon came.

[1] Margaret of Sylvester Judd's novel of that name (N. Y., 1845) and Miss Gabriel of Mary P. Smith's *Jolly Good Times at School* (N. Y., 1867).

[2] "The Schools of Olden Times" (anonymous) first appeared in THE MAINE FARMER near the beginning of the nineteenth century. Reprinted in Barnard's JOURNAL OF AMERICAN EDUCATION (Hartford, 1876), Vol. III, 419–421.

Her only recreation was the spelling match, and her chief opportunity leap-year:

> Alas, kind soul, though leap year came
> And went full many a time
> In single-blessedness she toiled
> Till far beyond her prime.

Life was a school to her, a school in which she learned all the rules well.

> But now indeed her toils were o'er
> Her lessons all are said,
> Her rules well learned, her words well-spelled
> She's gone up to the head.

This, certainly, is not poetry, but it shows one of the many attempts to make literary material of the school at a time when all literary effort was at a low ebb in America.

Since any intellectual accomplishments were thought inappropriate for women, female education was slow in developing in colonial New England.   Winthrop records the case of a woman who lost her wits by excessive reading, writing, and meddling with things "as are proper for men whose minds are stronger."[1]   Anne Bradstreet had to endure many sneers from her contemporaries, though she admitted the superior ability of men.   If we are to take as evidence the number of books published on education it would seem that the education of Indians and servants, white and black, was of greater concern than instruction for girls.[2]   This neglect may, no doubt, have been due to the fact that mothers were expected to train their daughters in household duties; hence manuals on

[1] Journal, op. cit., (April 13, 1645).

[2] Whitcomb, *Chronological Outlines of American Literature* (N. Y., 1893), 18–89.

home training were sent over from England.[1] Occasionally, as in the case of the Captain Daingerfield or Councilman Carter of Virginia,[2] private tutors were introduced into the home for the instruction of all the children.[3] The Old Latin Grammar school existed solely for boys. After the middle of the eighteenth century boarding schools were not uncommon for boys, though they were rare for girls.

Girls, however, were more inclined to keep diaries than boys so that a few of interest have come down to us from pioneer girls' boarding schools,[4] revealing the typical school life of reading, parsing, "flourishing" or writing, French, of instruction in embroidery and painting, as well as the life of the village in which the school is situated. Charlotte Sheldon in Miss Pierce School at Litchfield, Connecticut, read *Moral Tales* on Friday, May 13, 1796,—"attended meeting all day on Sunday" where she heard two very indifferent sermons. "Read the AMERICAN MAGAZINE in the afternoon, washed all forenoon Monday, sewed and began to work the edges of some ruffles. On Saturday, June 4, read in Goldsmith's animated nature and went to stores three times. Thursday, worked on shawl, studied a grammar lesson, parsed,

[1] *The Mother's Advice to Her Daughters*, a treatise on the education of ladies, imported 1766. See also Andrews, *Colonial Folkways* (New Haven, 1925), 144.

[2] *Journal and Letters of Philip Vickers Fithian*, Princeton Hist. So., 1903, records his experience as tutor in a Virginia home.

[3] *Colonial Folkways*, op. cit., 138.

[4] Harriette M. Forbes, *New England Diaries*, 1602–1800, privately printed 1923.

Emily N. Vanderpoel, *Chronicles of a Pioneer School* (Cambridge, Massachusetts, 1903), contains—diaries of Charlotte Sheldon, 1796; Julia Cowles, 1797; Mary Ann Bacon, 1802; Lucy Sheldon, 1801; Catherine Webb, 1815; Mary Wilbor, 1822; Caroline Chester, and Mary Peck, 1825.

read Cox's *Travels;* knit, read partly through *Macbeth,* one of Shakespeare's best tragedies . . . Friday 23, went to a ball, had a very agreeable one . . . Came home in the morning—Saturday 24, felt pretty dull. Sunday 25, read all the forenoon, attended meeting in the afternoon, heard very poor sermon . . . Thursday 29, knit, parsed, studied spelling."[1]

Some imaginary letters written by two boarding school girls just after they have returned home reveal much of their artificial and finical life in village and city.[2]   One of these letters from a city girl to her friend in the country is of special interest as showing not only the demand for Fielding and Smollett in novel reading but as disclosing the changing literary taste in the country:

Where are you, Harriet, and what are you doing?   Six months absent from the town!   What can you do to beguile the tedious hours?   Life must be a burden to you!   How can you enjoy yourself?   You have no plays, no card-parties, nor assemblies that are worth mentioning . . . A new novel may do something toward it!   I accordingly send you one, imported in the last ship. Foreign, to be sure; else it would not be worth attention.   They have attained a greater degree of refinement in the old world, than we have in the new; and are so perfectly acquainted with the passions, that there is something extremely amusing and interesting in their plots and counter-plots, operating in various ways, till the dear creatures are jumbled into matrimony in the prettiest manner that can be conceived.   We in this country are too much in the state of nature to write good novels yet.   An American novel is such a moral sentimental thing, that it is enough to give anyone the vapours to read one.[3]

Another girl, writing to her friend, agrees that Young's *Night Thoughts* are good emotional exercises, but that he

[1] *Chronicles of Pioneer School,* op. cit., 10–17.

[2] Hannah Webster Foster, *The Boarding School* (Boston, 1798), 140–236.

[3] Ibid., 156–157.

"tends to depress the spirit" with his gloominess. Thomson, on the other hand, is described as having elegance, sentiment, perspicuity, and even sublimity. "What an inimitable painter! How admirably he describes the infinitely variegated beauties and operations of nature."

If novels were imported from England for the pastime of frivolous young ladies, the education of females, too, was modelled after that of the mother country. Defoe, in lamenting the neglect of the education of women,[1] told of the kind of training they should be given:

> They should be taught all sorts of breeding suitable both to their genius and quality. And in particular, music and dancing, which it would be cruelty to bar the sex of because they are their darlings. But besides this, they should be taught languages, as particularly French and Italian, and I would venture the injury of giving a woman more tongues than one. They should, as a particular study, be taught all the graces of speech, and all the necessary air of conversation—'Tis the sordidest piece of folly and ingratitude in the world to withhold from the sex the due luster which the advantages of education give to the natural beauty of their minds.

By 1733 Charles Coffey's *The Boarding School* gave literary expression to this sort of education in comic opera.[2] Its plot, which has been repeated in farces down to the present time in both England and America, is that of a lovely young lady breaking away from the restraints of school life to elope with the dancing master.[3] But such material falls far short of serious dramatic interest and it did not attract early American writers in any

[1] Defoe, *An Essay upon Projects* (London, 1697).

[2] Coffey, Charles. *The Boarding School*, as it was performed at Theatre Royal in Drury-Lane (London, 1733).

[3] Barnard, W. B., *The Boarding School*, a farce (London and New York, 1841).

Also Miller, Alice Duer, *The Charm School* (N. Y., 1919).

form. Even had drama been in vogue in religious America at this time, it is probable that such a play as Coffey's would never have been tolerated; nor is it likely that a novel with such a plot would have found an audience in Puritan homes.

American writers on the subject of female education,—Benjamin Rush, Franklin, John Witherspoon, Joseph Dennie and Noah Webster—directed their efforts against the superficiality of such education. Rush held that America should break away from the European custom in this regard and should plan such a course for women as would aid them in the discharge of their duties as mothers of sons in a republic.[1] Franklin tersely protested against the partiality of parents who incurred lavish expense to give their daughters a fashionable education while their sons, upon whom they were often dependent for a subsistence, were kept in ignorance and at hard labor.[2] Webster, more emphatically, declared that young women should be trained in "what is useful," and that they should repair, especially, their deficiency in speaking and writing their own language, French being wholly unnecessary to their usefulness. He, too, complained that mechanics, shopkeepers, and even farmers who could at all afford it sent their daughters away to boarding schools in the larger towns where they would acquire music, drawing, dancing, and the "luxurious manners and amusements of England and France" while their sons were confined to the drudgery of shop

[1] Rush, Benjamin, *Essays.* "Thoughts upon Female Education Accommodated to the Present State of Society, Manners, and Government, in the United States of America" (Philadelphia, 1798), 71–83.

[2] Franklin, *Autobiography and Selections*, edited by H. A. Davidson (N. Y., 1908), 330. "A Petition of the Left Hand to Those Who Have the Superintendency of Education."

or field. By such a practice he asserts the daughters are educated above a connection with men in these occupations and domestic happiness is endangered in America.[1] There seemed to be an increasing consciousness on the part of these writers that America had a destiny of her own to fulfill and that education must prepare the way for this manifest destiny.

In the field of fiction two works on the education of girls are noteworthy in this period. The first, *The Power of Sympathy* (Boston, 1789) supposedly written by Sarah Wentworth Morton, is generally credited with the honor of being the first American novel. Written in the epistolary form of Richardson, it helped to break down the Puritan aversion to the English novels of the time by pleading the cause of female education. The other is *The Boarding School; or Lessons of a Preceptress to Her Pupils* by Hannah Webster Foster (Boston, 1798). "Sensible that much depends upon the early infusion of virtuous principles," the author attempts to cast her ideas on female deportment into some form by using the boarding school as the setting. Her volume, therefore, smacks of the didactic treatises and stories for children of Maria Edgeworth and thus belongs to the class of educational fiction.

The story is that of a clergyman's widow who, having two daughters of her own to educate in manners and morality, decides to take in seven other girls and start a school in her country home. The other girls, who came from the city, had already acquired the graces of fashionable deportment, but they still retained "juvenile eccentricities" which needed pruning. The widow, therefore, with all her prudence, sprightly

[1] Webster, Noah, *Essays.* "On Education of the Youth in America," (Boston, 1790) 27–30.

fancy, and cheerful disposition set about to domesticate
them, and to turn their thoughts toward the necessary
qualifications of home life. She declared that girls
who were bred

> ———————"to sing and dance,
> To dress, and troll the tongue, and roll the eye"

were utter nonentities. To this end she related a story
of the downfall after marriage of one girl who had been
given such an education, and of the success of another
who came finally to preside in a household with diligence,
neatness, and cheerfulness. She warned them away
from excessive novel reading and especially against
"immoral books of fiction, obscene conversation, immod-
est plays and cards—so much the taste of the present
day" among the fashionable.

In the year previous to *The Boarding School* Hannah
Foster had published *The Coquette* (1797) which, according to its title, showed the consequences to which a girl
trained in habitual coquetting is led. The work had a
tremendous vogue, running through thirteen editions
within forty years. It is probable that the story of the
widow's school in the instruction of morals was written to
offset the effect of the author's first work, but this
purpose of instruction kept her from making her second
book a creditable work of fiction. She at least, however,
felt the reaction against the sensibility, sentimentality,
and superficiality of the English education of women—a
reaction which Fitz-Greene Halleck later expressed in
what is perhaps his best poem.[1] Royall Tyler, another
of her contemporaries, enjoyed contrasting the foppish
manners of the city-bred girl who, taking her cue from
European society, strove by "hypocrisy to please"

[1] Halleck, Fitz-Greene, *Fanny* (N. Y., 1819) especially stanzas
XXI-XXII.

with the genuine sincerity and simple unaffectedness of our "free-born ancestors."[1]

In the survey of the beginnings of school life as a literary theme it was found that the old Latin Grammar school and the dame school, which were brought over from England and had been abundantly reflected in English literature, were the first to receive expression in America. The first accounts were merely an attempt to leave some record of the old educational life in the colonies, but, in the case of Winthrop, these were sufficiently representative of the culture and dignity of the man and of his times to have genuine literary interest for the historian of American prose. Education, being at this time the handmaid of the church, was based on a belief in the total depravity of man, and it depended to a large extent upon the rod of correction to get results. The popular reverence for certain old teachers led native versifiers to praise the schoolmaster's trade in ponderous and sober-minded eulogies and elegies appropriate to grammarian's funerals.

As the war for free thinking took on momentum in the colonies, as Franklin and his deistic friends turned their thoughts from monopolizing concern with eternal salvation to more practical matters, the attack upon the classics was begun. In the rising tide of enthusiasm for universal education in the nation, the inappropriateness of forcing the classics on all who desired to go to school was recognized, and was expressed in the literature dealing with school life. In the last quarter of the eighteenth century both the grammatical pabulum of the schools and the popular ignorance were satirized by the Hartford Wits and others. Likewise female education,

[1] See Tyler's, Introduction to *The Algerine Captive* (N. Y., 1797) and the prologue to *The Contrast* (N. Y., 1787).

which at first was the same as that which had arisen in
France and England, came in as the butt of ridicule.
Novel reading and the study of French were considered
inadequate training for women who were to be mates
of thrifty, free-born citizens in a republic.

CHAPTER IV

BACKGROUNDS OF ICHABOD CRANE

The school makes its first important appearance in American literature after the establishment of the district system for rural schools in New England. By the end of the eighteenth century "the little red schoolhouse" had become a tradition in New England and the Middle States and had brought along with it something of a literary flavor. It was in the district schoolmaster that our first American man of letters found material for creating an enduring character who, with the exception of Rip Van Winkle, may be said to be the first native American embodied in fiction. Several years' accumulation of literary protoplasm was necessary before the school could penetrate the American artistic imagination sufficiently to emerge distinctly as a theme in our literature. Even in the case of Irving the schoolmaster's relation to the school is described rather than narrated, and that briefly.

In colonial days nearly all life was rural. At the close of the eighteenth century less than four percent of the population lived in towns of eight thousand or over and only six towns and cities came within this class.[1] Though stages connected Boston, Albany, Providence, New York, and Philadelphia, travel was largely on horseback. Goodrich tells in his *Recollections* that there was only one chaise in the village of Ridgefield, Connecticut,

[1] Cubberley, *Rural Education in America*, Chapter I.

in 1800. "Such things were known in New York, Philadelphia and Boston, but the government had already laid a tax upon pleasure conveyances." Yet life in these cities was on a much lower plane of physical well-being than that of contemporary county seat towns. Garbage and litter were thrown in the streets for the accomodation of pigs, and skulls and feet of slaughtered animals lay on the shambles at the town's end. It was an agricultural era even in the cities.[1]

The district school system arose in New England as a response to the needs of the community, and the school of the district became the community undertaking as well as the care of the roads, the assessing of taxes, and the recruiting of the militia for which purposes the town had been divided. At first the school was moved about to different communities, being held a few weeks each year in each parish and at the center of the town, a practice not unusual in New England in 1725. Before the end of the century the districts were given legal right to elect the trustees, levy district school taxes, and select a teacher.[2] There was usually much dispute as to where the schoolhouse was to be located, but the custom was to select some worthless spot of ground near the geographical center of the district. Reminiscences of pre-Revolutionary days bear testimony that these houses were at first built of logs, though later they were weatherboarded and were frequently painted yellow or red. As late as 1800 "Peter Parley," writing of the schoolhouse in the little rural village of Ridgefield, Connecticut, says: "The schoolhouse consisted of rough, unpainted clapboards, upon a wooden frame. The chimney was of stone, and the fireplace was six feet wide and four feet deep. The

[1] Cobbett, A Year's Residence in America (London, 1819), 148.
[2] Cubberley, Public Education in the United States, 44.

flue was ample and so perpendicular that the rain and sleet fell direct to the hearth. In winter, the battle for life with green fizzling fuel, which was brought in sled lengths and cut up by the scholars, was a stern one . . .

"All around was bleak and desolate. Loose, squat stone walls, with innumerable breaches, inclosed the adjacent fields. A few tufts of elder, with here and there a patch of briars and pokeweeds flourished in the gravelly soil. Not a tree remained save an aged chestnut."[1]

Ichabod Crane's schoolhouse, though built of logs, had a pleasant location "at the foot of a woody hill with a brook running by." Its windows were "partly glazed and partly patched with leaves of old copy-books; its door is made secure in vacant hours by a withe twisted in the handle." Irving's picture is less real than Goodrich's. What he has to say of it is woven with the low murmur of pupil's voices conning over their lessons on drowsy summer days "interrupted now and then by the authoritative voice of the master in the tone of menace or command." He is more concerned with its setting beneath a formidable birch tree than the details of its appearance, all of which were presented in the light of the conscientious man who bore in mind the golden maxim: "Spare the rod and spoil the child." Ichabod Crane's scholars certainly were not spoiled.[2]

Once the district school had been established in New England it spread to all parts of the United States and flourished, especially during the fifty years just after the Revolution. In Massachusetts, when the law of 1789 raised the limitations for the maintenance of grammar

[1] Goodrich, N. Y., 1856, op. cit., 32–33.

[2] Mary C. Crawford, *Social Life in Old New England* (Boston, 1914), Chapter I.

schools to towns of two hundred families, it is said that
one hundred twenty towns were released from the obliga-
tion that had been established with the law of 1647.[1]
This change, while it gave rise to the academy, threw
also a greater burden upon the one-room school in the
smaller towns and rural districts of the state and increased
the importance of the rural schoolmaster, making him
the chief educational man in the community. It was
not until after 1789 that schools there were maintained
by general taxation. Boarding round in the rural districts
was of necessity part of the master's income. It was
the custom for rural teachers, who were at first usually
men, either to use the vocation as a stepping stone to
something higher or else, while they studied law or
medicine, to engage in other remunerative work during
the summer. Goodrich tells of a master "who had a
call for plowing, mowing, carting manure, etc., in summer,
and for teaching in winter, with a talent for music
at all seasons wherefore he became chorister upon occasions, when, peradventure Deacon Hawley could not
officiate." Cooper may have had such a character in
mind when he sketched his singing-master in *The Last
of the Mohicans*, and certainly this master is of the family
of Ichabod Crane who, though his story is said to have
been found in the posthumous papers of Diedrich
Knickerbocker, belongs to the period just after the
Revolution.[2]

The school life that was represented in the early
readers and spellers was a factor in helping to shape
the tradition. An original of the *New England Primer*
published about 1785 contains, just after the title page,

[1] G. H. Martin, *The Evolution of Massachusetts Public School
System* (N. Y., 1894), Lecture III.

[2] Irving says thirty years ago; that is, thirty years before 1819.

the following rhyme under which is the picture of two boys standing before the master:

> He who ne'er learns his A, B, C,
> Forever will a blockhead be;
> But he who to his books inclined
> Will soon a golden Treasure find.

And the lesson that was to be brought home from the letter "F" was that

> The Idle *Fool*
> Is whipt at school.[1]

Thus all through the early readers and spellers, wherever the school is mentioned, the good or the bad boy plays a prominent part, moral instruction being at all times the primary aim. With the publication of Noah Webster's *Speller* (1783) which was to replace Dilworth and others, stories illustrated by woodcuts and other factors of interest to children were added. This, too, marks the beginning of the spelling craze which before Mr. Webster's death had demanded 18,000,000 copies of his *Speller* and was to become an important phase of school tradition. If, as Mark Sullivan asserts,[2] the 122,000,000 copies of *McGuffey's Readers* scattered through the country had more to do in *our times* with forming the American mind than any of the so-called leaders of thought, it is no less probable that such men as Webster and Bingham did as much for an earlier generation. By 1824 with the publication in Boston of a new edition of *A Second Book for Reading and Spelling* by Samuel Worcester, playground activities and childhood sports and pastimes were beginning

[1] *The New England Primer* (Boston, C. 1790).
[2] Mark Sullivan, *Our Times*, Vol. II (N. Y., 1927) (*prope exordium*).

to figure in the text books.   This book contains woodcuts
of hoop rolling, of boys flying kites, of bubble blowing,
of an upset sleigh with the schoolchildren tumbling
out on the snow, of skating by moonlight, coasting,
and building sailing boats.   Worcester could not, however, resist the demand for moral instruction, and his
book followed its predecessors with stories of the good
and the bad boy.   Of special interest to us is the anecdote
of Dick Sly:[1]

Dick was a bright, active boy, a good scholar and
such a droll playfellow that he "would make you laugh
even if he treated you ill.   . . . When he was in school,
he was often tired of being still; and when his master
did not see him, he would make up faces or tickle those
who sat next to him, to make them laugh.   Then he
would look sober and grave, and be very busily studying
his lessons.   . . . It was a kind of hide and seek with
the teacher."   When at last, the boy was punished
for his tricks, the other scholars "were not glad to see
it."   Here was child psychology long before it was
added to college curricula.   Dick's mischievousness
had been mistaken for badness.

The popular compilations of Dyche, Perry, Dilworth—texts in wide use in America before the Revolution—contained almost nothing of school life and
very little reflection of child life.[2]   In Dilworth "A
Morning Prayer" for a child begins: "Lord grant that
the duties of this day be cheerfully undergone by me and
that I may be given grace to apply myself to learning
and that I may become a useful member of the common-
wealth.   Grant that I may be obedient to my parents

[1] Ibid., 71.

[2] Dilworth, *A New Guide to the English Tongue* (Philadelphia,
1818), 107.

and to those who have the care of my education and that I may lead an innocent and inoffensive life." Fleming's *The New Spelling Book* (London, 1825), another popular English speller of pre-Revolutionary days, contained many interesting cuts, one of which illustrates the story of some boys who went to the river to swim "instead of being at school." Smith, Brown, Jones and Robinson took it into their heads to play truant and go into the water. They had not been long in before Smith was drowned. . . . Brown's father followed the boys and lashed his son heartily, though nude. Jones and Robinson ran home half-dressed "where they were told that they would be sent to school for correction next day."

Webster declares that a good child will, when he gets up, "wash his hands and face clean; he will comb his hair and make haste to school; he will not play by the way as bad boys do. As for those boys and girls that mind not their books, and love not the church and school, but play with such as tell lies, curse, swear and steal, they will come to some bad end, and must be whipt till they mend their ways." *The Child's Instructor* (Philadelphia, 1808) contains a long reading lesson descriptive of boyhood in its worst form. "A bad boy is undutiful to his father and mother, disobedient and stubborn to his master, and ill-natured to all his playmates. He hates his books and takes no pleasure in improving himself in anything. He is sleepy and slothful in the morning, too idle to clean himself, and too wicked to say his prayers. He is always in mischief and will tell twenty lies in hope to clear himself. . . . He will steal whatever comes in his way. . . . In short he neglects everything that he should learn; by which means he becomes as he grows up a confirmed blockhead, incapable of anything but wickedness or folly, despised of all men of sense and virtue and generally dies a beggar."[1]

Next to the bad boy and closely akin to him, the lazy or idle boy looms large in these early readers, so eager were the first compilers to respond to the demand of the parents that diligence be "inculcated." *The Child's Guide* (Springfield, Massachusetts, 1837) tells a story of a boy who was so lazy that when he spelled "he drawled out one syllable after another as if he were afraid the syllables would quarrel. Once, when he was saying a lesson in Geography, his master asked him, "What is said of Hartford?" He answered, "Hartford is a flourishing comical town," without knowing what he was about. Leavitt's *Easy Lessons In Reading*[2] tells of a boy who was often either asleep in school or disturbing the study of others. "If you look in his desk, you would find it cluttered with acorn shells and apple parings. He would spend more time in catching flies and whittling cages for them, than in all his studies." All the instructor's efforts were in vain. His father took him from school and apprenticed him to the sea where he found a hard life. This is followed by the lines:

> I hate to be a boy! I do!
> This pile of books—I hate them too!
> I'll tear them all in tatters;
> Goodbye grammar:—Those boys are fools
> Who keep a book so full of rules,
> And all such tedious matters.
>
> Geography brimful of names
> One can't pronounce—now to disdain
> Such nonsense, I've a notion
> Old atlas! see! how I'll tear you,
> Across from China to Peru,
> And down the Atlantic Ocean.

[1] Johnson, *Old Time Schools and School Books*, op. cit., 237–8.
[2] (Boston, 1806, 1847), 24.

It will be remembered that Ichabod Crane, sitting enthroned on his lofty stool, had his desk piled high with "contraband articles and prohibited weapons" which had been detected on the persons of such idle urchins—half-munched apples, popguns, whirligigs, fly cages, and whole legions of rampant little paper game cocks.

Not all the instruction is negative, however, for there is the typically "Diligent Scholar," who, like Webster's good boy, never comes to school with dirty hands or uncombed hair. He hastens along the road with a ruddy, cheerful countenance bearing his small basket on his arm. He is never afraid of summer's heat or winter's cold, or a little rain or snow, but is usually there at the "fixed time." During the school hours he always stands or sits in his own place, and never reads any book "but such as his teacher tells him to read." He never stares at strangers when they visit the school and he pays attention to all his teacher says. He secretly rejoices when he learns a hard task, and when school is out he hurries home to help his father or mother.[1] Frequently the lazy and diligent scholars are contrasted as in the case of Charles and Henry in the *Child's Companion*.[2] Charles has gone no further than the word "absolute" in the speller,[3] while Henry has pushed on rapidly to the last page. The master has become tired of making complaints to Charles' parents, for they refuse to believe their boy is trifling. Henry, on the other hand, appreciates his opportunity because his parents have told him that many poor children cannot go to school.

With the Revolution the first step in the secularization of spellers and readers was taken, and the aphorisms of

[1] Rickets, *Juvenile Spelling Book* (Wheeling, Va. 1825), 158–161. Johnson, *Old Time Schools*, 215.

[2] Caleb Bingham (Boston, 1812), 14th edition, 71.

[3] Ibid., 20, Table VII.

Franklin were substituted for the Proverbs of Solomon; and "the tinsel glitter of Byron for the inspiring devotion of David."[1] French influences brought in by the war had made liberty, fraternity, and equality the watchwords in the place of duty and obedience, and "those pieces were deemed best by us grandsons of the Revolutionists which abounded in those glorious words."[2] *The New England Primer*, though abolished, was to continue in spirit for more than threescore years in the professedly moral stories of school readers—stories which were to "inculcate ideals" and to spur the youth from laziness to industry.[3]

John Pierpont, whose *National Reader* displaced Murray's *English Reader* in Boston in the autumn of 1829, was one of the first to recognize the merits of American poets and statesmen and to recommend readings from Webster, Irving, Bryant, Patrick Henry, and Jefferson, yet he follows his first lesson of "The Discovery of America" with two selections from English Literature: "The Good Scholar" by Edith J. May and "The Good Schoolmaster" by Thomas Fuller. With Murray, too, he continues the graveyard tradition of selections which began with the dialogue between Satan, Youth, and Christ in *The New England Primer*. One of the most terrorizing of these is "The School Boy," a verse reprint from *The Amulet:*[4]

> The School-Boy had been rambling all the day
> A careless, thoughtless idler,—till the night
> Came on, and warned him homeward . . .

[1] Martin, *Evolution of Massachusetts Public School System*, op. cit., 101–102.

[2] Warren Burton, *The District School As It Was* (Boston, 1907), 68.

[3] R. R. Reeder, *The Historical Development of School Readers* (N. Y., 1900), 20.

[4] John Pierpont, *The National Reader* (Boston, 1829), 266.

All day he had "sauntered lazily" in the meadows, but now darkness came rapidly over earth and sky. Now running breathlessly, now "whistling to keep his courage up," he passed by accident into the wicket gate which led into the village churchyard. Here were dark tall cypresses where bats darting about added to the terror, and he fancied "shapeless forms came flitting by him." Presently overcome with fear he sank down and gazed wildly about him till his eyes fell upon the inscription on a tomb which told how time flies and death pursues. From the grave there seemed to rise a voice telling him of time misspent, of death approaching rapidly and of the dark eternity that followed. He fainted and lay there senseless on the ground until his frantic mother found him. From this fearful hour a strange influence came over his life. He became a thoughtful, industrious boy, and never played truant again. Now that he is a man he writes these "feeble lines" that other boys may be warned.

Caleb Bingham, who was himself a schoolmaster and writer of the first *Young Ladies Accidence in America,* compiled three school books as well known as Webster's— *The Child's Spelling Book, The Columbian Orator,* and *The American Preceptor.* They were rich not only in selections of patriotic fervor and native American material, but contained, as compared with other spellers and readers, a wealth of material dealing with child life at home and at school. Best known of these selections, which Bingham made known to the public, was[1] "Lines Spoken at a School Exhibition by a Little Boy Seven Years Old," written by David Everett, another schoolmaster, for one of his pupils. It was echoed at school exhibitions for two generations, being alluded to in such

[1] *The Columbian Orator* (Boston, 1807), 8th edition, 57.

a circumstance in 1833 in Burton's *District School As It Was*, in 1874 in Mary P. Smith's *Jolly Good Times at School*, and in 1926 in Hewin's *A Mid-century Child and Her Books*. So popular were these lines that Edward Everett in a speech at Cambridge once referred to it as a "favorite poem, which many persons have done the honor to ascribe to me, but which was in reality written by a distant relative and namesake of mine, and, if I mistake not, before I was born."[1]

> You'd scarce expect one of my age,
> To speak in public on the stage;
> And if I chance to fall below
> Demosthenes and Cicero,
> Don't view me with a critic's eye
> But pass my imperfections by.

The poem is interesting from many points of view. It breathes the patriotic fervor of the time, and reflects the consciousness of the rising glory of the colonies, the rivalry with the mother country, and the early rivalry of the states. Most of all it reveals the secret love of power so dominent in colonial life, and the related passion for improvement. Boys on exhibition days were supposed to display their improvements.

> Large streams from little fountains flow
> Tall oaks from little acorns grow . . .
>
> Where's the boy, but three feet high
> Who's made improvements more than I?
> These thoughts inspire my youthful mind
> To be the *greatest of mankind;*
> Great, not like Caesar, stained with blood;
> But only great as I am good.

Power and goodness, even power through goodness,— these were dominant notes in colonial New England.

[1] Duyckinck, Vol. I, 568.

If a poem may be meritorious from its popularity or from the truth in reflecting what is in the minds of the people on a popular occasion, this would deserve a place in the history of American literature, for it is probable that not even Lincoln at Gettysburg spoke out of the minds of the people more than this youthful orator.

One other selection from Bingham should be noted as important in imaging the life of a primitive Ichabod. The scene, in a wayside tavern, presents both the propensity of the itinerant schoolmaster[1] for drink and his general illiteracy as well as the local tendency to hire a cheap one.

Enter schoolmaster, *with a pack on his back.*

SCHOOLMASTER: How fare you, landlord? What have you got that's good to drink?

LANDLORD: I have gin, West-India, genuine New England, whiskey, and cider brandy.

SCHOOLMASTER: Make us a stiff mug of sling. Put in a gill and a half of your New England; and sweeten it well with lasses.

LANDLORD: It shall be done, Sir, to your liking.

Through this conversation at the bar, the schoolmaster finds there is a vacancy in the district school and that the committeemen will soon be there to talk the matter over. He learns from the landlord that the former master was a "tyrant of a fellow and very extravagant in his price. He grew so important the latter part of his time, that he had the frontery to demand ten dollars a month and his board." What is more he has been so busy "poring over his books," that he has failed to patronize the landlord's tavern. Finally, his severity of discipline has swung the tide of public opinion and he has been hooted out of town. The itinerant master admits that he has

[1] *The Columbian Orator* (Hartford, 1807), 158–165.

had only one year of schooling but is no less proud of his accomplishments. He can read a newspaper without spelling more than half of the words, can "write considerably" and "cipher as fur as division." Best of all he will teach for five dollars a month. This saving so pleases the committee that he is hired outright over the parson's dissenting vote.[1]

A detailed study of the various representations of the school in all the early readers is forbidden here by consideration of space. The didactic Murray readers, which came into popularity early in the century, contained practically nothing of school life; yet the first of the "didactic pieces" in his *English Reader* is a selection from Addison on "The Importance of a Good Education," beginning: "I consider the human soul without education, like marble in a quarry."[2]   In general it is in the primary readers that school and child life are best represented, attempts being made by men like Bingham to appeal to the young through such media. This Herbartian appeal was utilized later by the best of the children's magazines—YOUTH'S COMPANION, ST. NICHOLAS, and OUR YOUNG FOLKS, which took pride in their interest in child life.

Next to the readers, spellers, and orators perhaps in importance in fostering the development of the conception of the rural school as a literary theme are the farmer's almanacs.   "No one," says Tyler,[3] "who would penetrate to the core of the early American literature, and would read in it the secret history of the people in whose minds it took root, and from whose minds it grew, may not by any means turn aside in lofty scorn from the

---

[1] Cited in Johnson op. cit., 280.

[2] L. Murray, *The English Reader* (N. Y., 1843), 64.

[3] Moses Coit Tyler (N. Y., 1878), op. cit., Vol. II, 120–130.

almanac . . . the supreme and only necessity even in households where the Bible and the newspaper are still undeserved or unattainable luxuries." About the close of the seventeenth century, with the establishing of printing presses in many parts of the colonies, the publication of the almanac was no longer restricted to any particular locality, and following close upon Cambridge, Boston became early celebrated for the number and variety of these publications and the intellectual attainments of their authors. Nathaniel Ames of Dedham, Massachusetts, published an almanac annually for thirty-eight years (1726–1764) when, upon his death, it was continued by his son. Isaiah Thomas' NEW ENGLAND ALMANAC appeared in 1775 and continued for forty-two years, approaching *Poor Richard* in wit and useful hints to farmers.

Not least among these useful hints to the farmer were those pertaining to his school. Very often they satirized his provincial ignorance and illiteracy. Ames, who had a sincere passion for public education, frequently referred to the school and education. In the July (1743) number we find: "Rich men without wisdom and learning are called sheep with Golden Fleeces;" in September: "Ignorance has the most confidence;" in December, 1731: "For shallow brains think all that's hard and high, unlawful and impossibility." In July, 1764, comes a pungent comment on Commencement at Cambridge:

> *Much talk and nothing said*
> Much money sunk
> Much liquor drunk.

In 1746 he prints at length a lively dialogue between a scholarly schoolmaster and a clown which both satirizes provincial ignorance and idealizes education:

CLOWN: Why my neighbor Vulcan put his son out to Coledge to learn to be a minister, he was an honest lad, and used to speak the truth, but now he tells me the world turns round and that the stars stand stock still in the skies. He says too that all the scholards and ministers believe that the world turns round, for my part I think the ministers ought to be turned out of the pulpits if they maintain such wicked Doctrines; but the question is this, whether you don't read conjuring Books at Coledge that bewitches you into such an opinion.

The master replies that the advantages of a college education lead one to see the reasonableness of such a theory, and leaves the bumpkin prating of his own superior knowledge of geese and cows.

This clown was just such a Jonathan as appeared in Thomas Green Fessenden's "The Country Lovers or Mr. Jonathan Jolthead's Courtship with Miss Sally Snapper: An Excellent new Song, said to be written by its author; and really founded on Fact." (Tune—Yankee Doodle.) After telling of his coming of age and his determination to go courting we get a brief survey of his school life:

> Moreover, sir, I'd have you know
> That he had got some knowledge,
> Enough for common use, I trow
> But had not been to college.
>
> A hundred he could count 'tis said
> And in the Bible read, sir,
> And by good Christian parents bred
> Could even say the creed, sir.
>
> He'd been to school to Master Drawl
> To spell a- bom- in- a- ble,
> And when he missed, he had to crawl,
> Straight under master's table.[1]

[1] Thomas Green Fessenden, *Original Poems* (N. Y., 1804). Duyckinck, Vol. I, 595.

Royall Tyler joined with Fessenden and the almanac-makers in laughter over the simplicity of agricultural America. Both he and Fessenden contributed humorous poems to Joseph Dennie's FARMER'S WEEKLY MUSEUM. His poem "The Bookworm" satirizes slavish devotion to the classics as well as general stupidity. His Jonathan of *The Contrast* (N. Y., 1787) belongs to the same family of Joltheads and they in turn were closely related to the Ichabods.

The almanac which keeps the subject of schools and education constantly before the people was THE FARMER'S ALMANACK. Its Farmer's Calendar for every month in the year contained not only useful, but entertaining matter in the form of familiar essays, and brief "paragraphs." No subject interested the Thomases more than to satirize the stinginess of the Yankee farmers in the payment of country schoolmasters, a parsimony which the Thomases argued could only secure the incompetent for the instruction of their children. For November, 1820, we read:

This is the last month of autumn and it is now the business of the prudent man to be making his calculations about winter matters. I have often mentioned the importance of schooling the rising generation. Few, if any, countries are blessed like New England with public school establishments. No stinginess about the business. See that you have an able master and pay him well. Here my neighbor and I can never agree; for he says: "So much of this here larnin is altogether useless and expensive. There is Joe Simple—good enough for our school. He has cyphered through compound interest and that's fur enough for any man. He knows nothing about jogrify and grammar and such stuff; but he can write as good a hand as I can; and as for reading, he is far better than Squire Puff. In spelling they say he is a curiosity. I have often heard that when he was a boy he could spell Nebuchadnezzar quicker than any one in school. I move, Mr. Cheerman, that we hire Joe Simple to keep our school this winter, give him five dollars a month and board himself, which is all he axes."

Joe Simple is only another name for the schoolmaster who chatted with the landlord in the wayside tavern and for him who flogged the tough-headed, "broad-skirted Dutch urchins." Repeatedly the Farmer's Calendar warned that a "cheap schoolmaster makes a dear school."[1] "I hope you have hired a good schoolmaster, for a poor one is a nuisance to the neighborhood."

NOVEMBER, 1804: "Now let the noise of your flail awake your drowsy neighbor. Bank up your cellars. Now hire a good schoolmaster and send your children to school as much as possible."
DECEMBER 1815: "It is all important now that you send your children to school; but take care that you have a good instructor for them. It is not every one who apes the gentlemen that is fit to this undertaking. To strut in white top boots, brandish a cane, drink brandy, smoke segers, are not the most essential qualifications for a schoolmaster. It is a serious misfortune that in many parts of our country schools are exceedingly neglected; and it would seem that were it not for the laws obliging them to have at least the appearance of schools there would be no provision at all for this purpose made for years! What better estate can you give your offspring than a good education? I would urge you to send them to college. . . . See that you have the best teachers in your town schools; be not stingy about the price."

The spirit of the old New England winter breathes throughout the autumn and winter months of the Calendar. That spirit, mingled with the general interests in schools and schoolmasters, was caught up later by Whittier and put into lasting form. The Calendar of December, 1819, carries an admonition in the gale:

Here it comes again! Bluster, bluster, bluster!
Well, we have been preparing for it. . . . Kill your hogs for home use, and be careful about smoking your hams, for every farmer should endeavor well to save his bacon.

[1] THE NEW ENGLAND ALMANAC (Boston, December, 1818). For a very complete collection of these almanacs see Columbia University Library.

All things go nicely—the boys and girls are at school—the cattle are well fed and carded—the linters are cleaned—there is plenty of wood for the women. Come, neighbor Jenkins, let's you and I take a game of checkers for love and good will.

The *Letters* of St. John de Crèvecœur with their insistence upon thrift, their love of the land, their care for domestic and wild animals, their faith in the future of America and with their intimate and authoritative insight into eighteenth century American life, seem permeated with the spirit of the old farmers' almanacs.[1] "The Snowstorm," recently brought to light, has the charm both of Virgil's "Georgics" and of Horace's "Ode to Winter."[2] Mingled with the author's tenderness and pity for his oxen and horses and his haste to throw open the bars that they may come in out of the storm is his anxiety for the children at the district school. Tom, the negro boy, mounts the family mare bare-back and soon the schoolhouse appears through the blinding storm, "at the door of which each child is impatiently waiting." All three of the children pile on, one before and two behind and seeing that Rachel, the widow's daughter, is about to be left without assistance, they quickly make a place for her. Then turning about and boldly facing the wind, Bonny, the faithful mare, brings her valuable cargo surely and safely to port by a roaring hearth fire where a feast of "milk-biscuit, short-cake, and newly baked apple-pies" is prepared. This is not only an unforgettable picture of school life, but it foreshadows the work of Sarah Orne Jewett, (*A Native of Winby*) Whitcomb Riley, and Hamlin Garland in picturing with loving detail

[1] Crèvecœur, *Eighteenth Century Sketches* (Yale Press, 1925), 39–51.

[2] Horace Bennett, "Winter Without Bids Us Make Merry Within," Bk. I, *Odes and Epodes* (N. Y., 1908), 13.

the life of humbler people in their battle with the environment. It was this old battle with winter that made the compiler of *The Child's Spellingbook* (Bingham, Hartford, 1798, p. 32) include the following sentences for children to read:

How cold it is! Where are the little girls and boys? Have they not yet come from school? Here they come, here they come. . . . Who was at the head of the class today? Rachel . . .

This is winter. Well, never mind it. We will sit by the fire and read, and tell stories, and look at pictures.

Take care, little boy, you stand too near the fire. You will burn your shoes. . . . Dinner is ready. Come, little frozen boys, come get some pudding.

These winters, as Goodrich reminds us, were accompanied by many hindrances and drawbacks for school children not only from the harsh rod of disciplinary constraint, but from colds and pneumonia, mumps and measles, whooping-cough and "that scourge and terror of the world" small-pox. The rural schoolhouse, with its broken windowpanes, its open floors and walls, its rude stove or open fireplace only added insult to injury. One frontier schoolmaster, when his trustees became desultory in furnishing wood, was rudely dismissed for allowing the older boys to kindle the fire from the slabs off the side of the house. He refused to cut the wood himself, since it was a part of his contract that the trustees should furnish it.[1]

While Crèvecœur and certain compilers of school readers were exhibiting a sympathy for child life, there were two other writers whose sympathies were quite elsewhere than with the children. They are chiefly concerned with the hard lot of the schoolmaster. One of these, Royall

[1] C. Thomas, *The Frontier Schoolmaster* (Montreal, 1880), 34.

Tyler, whose character in *The Algerine Captive* happily escaped from teaching a rural school to fall into the hands of pirates, brought out his book in 1798,[1] and the other, Alexander Wilson, whose *"Forresters"* gives a very clear picture of a rural school and of its master, published his poem in the PORTFOLIO in the same year in which Irving's *Knickerbocker History* appeared (1809).

If we may trust the point of view in *The Algerine Captive* as his own, Tyler's reaction against rural teaching as well as that to the school curriculum of his day is as emphatic as it is vivid. In his preface the author calls attention to the great change that has taken place in the American reading public to books that are inclined to amuse rather than to instruct. This was made possible in America, he asserts, through the fact that so many people have been taught to read, a task which in New England had already been half accomplished. No sooner was a taste for amusing literature diffused than all orders of country life forsook the sober sermons and practical pieties of their fathers for the gay stories and splendid impieties of the traveller and the novelist. He deplores the fact not only that Mrs. Radcliffe's hobgobblins and haunted houses were "not of our own manufacture," but that her novels and other imported works of fiction depict the manners and customs of a strange country, "rendering our home-spun habits disgusting." He decides that there are two things wanting in America: "That we write our own books of amusement," and that we exhibit our own manners in them; and concludes, therefore, to write an autobiographical novel the first part of which at least *"would display a portrait of New England manners hitherto unattained."*

[1] Royall Tyler, *The Algerine Captive, or The Adventures of Doctor Updike Underhill* (Walpole, New Hampshire, June, 1797).

In the chapters of the book dealing with the childhood education of Captain Updike Underhill and his preparation for college, and especially the chapter in which the hero "keepeth a country school," Tyler exhibits a vividness and truth to detail that are hardly surpassed by the best of Richard Malcom Johnston's stories of school life. This realism, with the ingenuity in the thought, caused at least one eminent critic to lament that Tyler's book had fallen into neglect.[1]

Young Updike Underhill, the hero, was no Ichabod. In his twelfth year the minister, who went to his district to make his annual inspection of schools, and incidentally to trade for oxen, found in him superior ability and urged that he be sent to college. When the father pleaded poverty, the mother joined with the minister, saying she would work her fingers to the bone to permit it, confident that he would make a preacher as "much run after as the great Mr. Whitefield."[2] He therefore prepared for college with the minister and at the annual convention declaimed his four hundred lines from Homer to the great satisfaction of the clergymen present, who esteemed "dead language more than the living." One gravely declared that he knew General Washington read Greek, else he should never have overcome the Hessians at Trenton. The agricultural father, however, was by no means certain of this, but maintained that all that was useful in the Greek language had been translated and that legislatures should interfere with such wasteful teaching. He declared emphatically that ministers only taught these defunct languages because they knew nothing else.

[1] Duyckinck, Vol. I, 416. See also Van Doren, *The American Novel*, 8–10.

[2] Royall Tyler, op. cit., 56.

The boy, nevertheless, was now qualified to teach a country school and by the recommendation of the minister was engaged to teach such a school as soon as the fall work was over. All during the summer his head was filled with "the anticipations, pleasures and profits of a pedagogue." In the fields he "stood suspended over his dung fork" thinking of his scholars seated in awful silence around him, of how he would rule them by love instead of by manual corrections, and how he would have an opportunity to indulge himself with his favorite Greek. But in a short time he found himself at the head of a school of sixty scholars, four of whom were overgrown boys of eighteen. "The generality of them were under the age of seven. Perhaps a more ragged, ill bred, ignorant set, never were collected for the punishment of a poor pedagogue."[1]

Instead of the silence anticipated, there was incessant clamor interspersed with questions: "Sir, may I read?" "May I spell?" "Master, may I go out?" "Will the master mend my pen?" One of the larger boys whom he found it necessary to punish returned to school bringing his father, a tall raw-boned man, who brandished an ox whip and "vowed he would whip the skin from his bones." This was the only instance of the "overwhelming gratitude of parents" which he had dreamed of. Moreover, the village gossip circulated untruthful tales about him. So gross was the stupidity of the community that he could find no companionship, not even among the "cornfed nymphs" at the quilting bee who only stared at him when he mentioned Ulysses or Penelope. To cap the climax, his pay, which was to be four dollars a month and board, he found was not to be expected until the following autumn and "then not in

[1] Ibid., 60.

cash, but produce." He was to become his own collector and pick up his dues, half a peck of corn or rye in a place. Lucky it was for him when the joyful news came that one of the thoughtless boys had burnt down the schoolhouse. This fire put an unexpected end to his distress, though the common cry was that he should pay the loss since his laxity had encouraged carelessness. As a prodigal he then returned to his father, who received him kindly, and to his mother, who had fearful dreams that he had fallen into the hands of savages.

Another work which deserves more consideration than it has hitherto received is that of the pioneer American ornithologist, Alexander Wilson. Arriving from his native Scotland in 1794, he taught in Pennsylvania for a decade. In October, 1804, he set out on foot to Niagara Falls, returning in December through snow "mid-leg deep" after a journey of twelve hundred fifty-seven miles and an absence of fifty-nine days. The result of this excursion was *The Forresters*, a fine, Goldsmithlike descriptive poem in rhymed couplets.[1]

Declaring that American scenery is seldom the theme of poetry, whereas there is scarcely a hillock or stream of England that does not live in immortal song, he passes before our eyes images of American life on the frontier. Student of nature as he is, birds and forest attract him most, but, true to the eighteenth century love of towns, his interest in people, taverns, Dutch, German, and other backwoods settlements is hardly secondary. Emerging

---

[1] *The Poems and Literary Prose of Alexander Wilson, The American Ornithologist, for the First Time Fully Collected and Edited and Compared with the Original Early Editions, Mss., Etc.* With memorial introduction, essays, notes, by Rev. Alexander B. Grossart. Paisley: Alexander Gardener, 1876, Vol. II, *Poems.* "The Frontier," 111–173.

from the "dull woods," he pauses to contemplate pastoral farms and landscapes:

> Where various sounds of human toil were heard;
> There round a hut, upon a sloping green,
> Gay laughing bands of playful boys were seen;
> Soon "Books," aloud is thundered from the door,
> And balls and hoops must charm the hours no more.

With awe he and his companions enter the "sequestered shed" while all eyes turn the "strangers to survey." The master, grave and courteous, rises, bows with meekness, and offers them a seat. Then looking round he

> . . . bids, by signs alternate classes rise,
> Hears, reads, instructs, with solemn voice and slow,—
> Deep busy silence muffling all below;
> Slates, pens, and copy-books in order pass,
> And peace and industry pervade each class.
> Dear to the muse, to Truth, to Science dear,
> Be he who humbly toils and teaches here!
> His worth, his labours shall not be forgot,
> And thus the muse records them as she ought.[1]

Then for three score lines he expresses the keenest sympathy for the hard lot of the rural schoolmaster who, though he leads the growing mind "From humble A, B, C, to God's own page," is condemned to bear daily the taunts of ungrateful and partial parents, and to endure

> . . . the idle dull,
> The blockhead's dark impenetrable skull—
> The endless round of A, B, C's whole train,
> Repeated o'er ten thousand times in vain.

Heaped upon this is the gossip of children to believing parents: "Our lazy master loves his ease. The boys at

[1] Ibid., 120; 295–320.

school do anything they please." This, together with the
grudging look from those who pay him his little sum,
makes the poet pray to just Heaven "to give them
[rural schoolmasters], health and fortitude of soul."
So closely does Wilson follow Tyler's account of the
experience of the schoolmaster that one is led to believe
he had read *The Algerine Captive*, the acquaintance
of which is likely since he and Tyler were both
contributors to the PORTFOLIO. But whatever may be
said of his source, one critic in 1854 thought the work
important enough in the cause of education to suggest
that it be printed for gratuitous circulation in every
village or school district in the country.[1] The lines
as a whole suggest Crabbe, who like him, felt sharply the
drudgery of teaching as he saw it in his native village.

Another eclogue of "The Country School," contributed
anonymously to the NEW HAMPSHIRE SPY and preserved
in E. H. Smith's collection of American Poems[2] presents
a dramatic situation at the school house strikingly like
that of Ichabod Crane. The poet devotes its entire one
hundred lines to the proceedings within the schoolhouse
for one whole day, beginning:

> Put to the door—the schools begun—
> Stand in your places every one,—
> Attend! . . .
> Read in the Bible,—tell the place,—
> Job twentieth and seventh verse—
> Caleb, begin.   And— he— shall— suck . . .

[1] Duyckinck, op. cit., 550.

[2] See New Hampshire Historical Collection for NEW HAMPSHIRE
SPY, 1792. See also E. H. Smith, *American Poems* (N. Y., 1793).
Stedman and Hutchinson, Vol. IV, 127. *The Columbian Muse*,
Printed by Matthew Carey (Philadelphia, 1794), 219. Barnard,
AMERICAN JOURNAL OF EDUCATION, Vol. V, 189.

Caleb continues laboriously while the teacher's promptings are interrupted by one boy's sticking a pin in another. Turning from the Bible reading class in disgust, the schoolmaster mends pens, sets copies, examines sums simultaneously with answering requests to leave the room, giving an order for more wood to be brought, and inquiring into the cause of some strange noise. The day is one of continuous attempts to hear recitations broken by numberless interruptions and suspensions. While Billy tries to read from his speller, one boy snatches another's ruler, one's nose bleeds, another leaves his seat, and still another must be corrected for coming to school with dirty hands.

Fortunately, as the grammar class was being drilled in punctuation, a visitor knocks, calls the teacher outside, and invites him to dismiss his "brain-distracting crew" and prepare to come to a dance that night. Fiddle and fiddler will be there. Then follows bedlam in which the master brings his day to a swift dramatic close.

> Silence. The second class must read,
> As quick as possible—proceed,
> Not found your book yet? Stand—befix'd—
> The next read, stop—the next—the next,
> You need not read again, 'tis well.
> Come, Tom and Dick, choose sides to spell
> Will this word do? Yes. Tom spell *dunce*.
> Sit still there all you little ones.
> I've got a word,—well, name it. *Gizzard*.
> You spell it, Sampson g—i—z
> Spell *conscience*, Jack. k—o—n
> S—h—u—n—t—s. Well done!
> Put out the next—*Mine is folks*.
> Tim, spell it—P—h—o—u—x.
> O shocking! Have you all tried? No.
> Say master, but no matter, go—
> Lay by your books—and you, Josiah,
> Help Jed to make the morning fire.

The master's making *Josiah* rhyme with *fire* and *verse*
with *place* was, no doubt, a case in which he allowed
provincial usage to outweigh standard English, or
perhaps it may have been the pressure of the situation
that caused him to lapse.

With Irving it is the schoolmaster in love that makes
the real theme of his story. He weaves his character
skillfully into the mellow light of Dutch tradition, giving
him a setting not of the schoolroom only, but of the
community. It is Ichabod's conflict with those burly,
rustic admirers of Katrina Van Tassel that brought about
his undoing. The school is reflected only in the light of
his love adventure, for only once do we get a peep inside
his "little literary realm" where he sat enthroned with
the contraband articles and prohibited weapons lying on
the desk before him. This is at the moment when the
negro boy appears with the Van Tassel invitation to the
"quilting frolic" that evening. Austere dominion then
gives place to hubbub; lessons are hurriedly and care-
lessly recited with impunity. Any one who was not
quick, received "a smart application in the rear to help
him over a tall word." Books were flung aside without
being put away on the shelves, inkstands were over-
turned, benches were thrown down, and the whole school
was turned loose an hour before the usual time, bursting
forth like a legion of young imps, yelping and racketing
about the green in joy at their early emancipation. After
a careful toilet before the broken mirror that hung in the
schoolhouse, Ichabod fares forth, a knight-errant in
quest of adventure, a Don Quixote astride his
Gunpowder.

Like Goldsmith's schoolmaster, Ichabod was thought
inferior in learning only to the parson; notwithstanding
his chief erudition was based upon psalmody, Mather's

History of New England Witchcraft, the NEW ENGLAND ALMANAC, and a book of dreams and fortune-telling—all of which he drew upon to the delight and wonder of country damsels. It was this that stirred the jealousy of country bumpkins and led Brom Bones to use witchcraft as his *modus operandi* in the dénouement. But whatever we may say of our hero's gulping awkwardness and bewitching stupidity, we shall have to recognize in him a certain amount of *savoir faire* which enabled him to get along with housewives and farmers in out-of-school hours. In the homes of his pupils he laid aside his peculiarly austere dignity "and became wonderfully gentle and ingratiating," rendering himself both useful and agreeable. Not only did he assist the fathers in the lighter labors of the farm such as taking horses to water, mending fences, driving cows to the pasture, and cutting kindling, but "he found favor in eyes of mothers by petting children, particularly the youngest; and like the lion bold, which whilom so magnanimously the lamb did hold [See *The New England Primer*, the letter L] he would sit with a child on one knee and rock a cradle with his foot for whole hours together." If he does not ostensibly reveal the sense of humor so necessary to a schoolmaster, he does exhibit a tact in his vital connections with parents that is a goal not yet reached in modern Parent Teacher Associations.[1]

Not all colonial schoolmasters who boarded round fared so sumptuously as he. Like Pinch of Shakespeare's play, he was naturally a lean-faced, hungry soul. He, therefore, gulped with satisfaction when he looked upon the groaning Dutch board where ducks and geese swam

[1] The custom of boarding round was practiced in other parts of the world. See Matthai, *Village Government in British India* (London, 1916), 49.

in their own gravy.   Even as he rolled his eyes over the fat meadow lands, he was enraptured with anticipation, for his gastronomical soul overreached his poetic soul and the beauties of the farm were interpreted in terms of the bounties of the table.   Perhaps, too, could he win the heiress, Katrina, his eager soul might be fed to satisfaction and the endless drudgery of teaching would be over.   The frontier schoolmaster of Vermont who complained in his diary of cold gander for breakfast every day in the week had no such anticipations.[1]   William Austin, a New England schoolmaster of Ichabod's time who turned lawyer and became the "creator of Peter Rugg," makes the hard fare the entire motive of his humorously fantastic story, *The Sufferings of a Country Schoolmaster* (1825).   Starvation, too, seems to be the theme[2] of the *Confessions of a Country Schoolmaster*.[3] Unless they were married and boarded themselves, teachers of the "old field school" on Southern plantations apparently fared better than these New England rural pedagogues.

In the survey we have been making of the school life in the early literature of America, we find evidence that by the time Irving came to write, "the little red schoolhouse" and its master had been established as a tradition with something of a literary flavor.   Incidental though it is, it is nevertheless insistent.   No epics or tragedies, no novels or short stories, and only a few poems worthy of mention were found.   The reasons for this are obvious: first, that none of these forms of literature had very emphatically been introduced in America up to this time;

[1] *The Frontier Schoolmaster*, op. cit., 1880, Chapter I.

[2] Austin, James W., *Literary Papers of William Austin* (Boston, 1895), 99–119.

[3] BOSTON MONTHLY MAGAZINE, June, 1826.

and, second, that child life and the life of the humbler folk had not yet become widely used as material for literature. In an age of satire such as the eighteenth century, the school drew its share of sparks from the wits of the day. The artificiality of female education, the study of ancient tongues to the neglect of the mother tongue, the severe discipline, and the ignorance both of the people and of the schoolmaster made excellent targets for those who were impatient of America's provincialism.

It is doubtful whether the school, though a "little world," can ever be the setting for the themes of love, death, and heroism which are so common in literature. Though Romeo and Juliet were children, their love required a larger sphere of activity than the schoolroom. They were adults living in an age of romance. The time may come when some dramatist may realize childhood to such a degree that he may treat this "little world" as a real and tragic world. The eighteenth century was an adult world; even its greatest books for children were written perhaps without a thought of children—*Gulliver's Travels* and *Robinson Crusoe*. Fragmentary and interpolated as the early literature of school life was in this century, it seems probable that with the awakening of interest in education and child life that came in the nineteenth century, a more vigorous attempt would be made to use the school as literary material. After the flowering of the short story in Irving which is, perhaps, best illustrated by his story of the schoolmaster, after the migration of Goldsmith and other romantics to America, the way seems clear for an ampler expansion of this tradition in our literature. But time elapses between Irving's schoolmaster and the beginning of the literary and educational renaissance. American intellectual culture seemed exhausted after the wars with the mother country. Making a living was the chief occupation. Forests had to be cleared and houses and roads built before the people could sit by the fire and read with any composure.

CHAPTER V

FROM SLEEPY HOLLOW TO FLAT CREEK

The period from Irving's *Sketch Book* to the publication of *The Hoosier Schoolmaster* marks the time when the common school reached perhaps its highest place in the public mind. Before this half century has elapsed, many changes have taken place both in literary and educational history as well as in the history of the nation at large. During this time our greatest literary figures were to come upon the scene, and though the center was chiefly Boston, the work of the last decade pointed toward a second "discovery of America" which was to bring with it the laughter of the West and South.[1] This was the time also in which the great battle for free schools occurred, led by such men as James G. Carter, Horace Mann, and Henry Barnard who had caught some of the new enthusiasm for education from the protestant countries of Europe. In 1839 the first State Normal school was established at Lexington, Massachusetts, some of whose graduates became teachers in the backwoods of Ohio and Indiana. By 1860 twelve normal schools had been set up in nine states extending from Maine to Minnesota and six private schools were being conducted with the same purpose.[2] Meanwhile Henry Barnard organized the first of the teachers' institutes in America (1839) and they were introduced into Ohio in 1845, into

[1] Pattee, *History of American Literature Since* 1870, Chap. I–II.
[2] Cubberley, *Public Education in the United States*, 293.

New Hampshire, Vermont, and Indiana in 1846, Maine in 1847, Wisconsin in 1848, and Iowa in 1853.[1] That the second work of fiction dealing largely with the school should come from Vermont, bearing the copyright date of 1847, is significant.[2] If the rural school is to find a place as a theme in American literature, we should expect this to occur during the period from 1825–1875— the half century of the great common school revival.

The two decades following the appearance of *The Legend of Sleepy Hollow* were a period in which the collecting of old traditions became a fad. Since it was the era of good feeling, of spread-eagle oratory, and of national expansion, it has been referred to as a time of "flamboyant Americanism in our native literature."[3] Though Irving had taught Americans to look for legends in their own country, he himself now turned for the most part away from native material to the more romantic life of Columbus and to tales of Granada and the Alhambra. In 1836 and 1837, it is true, he returned to the American scene in *Astoria* and *The Adventures of Captain Bonneville*, but they are cursorily written and they do not reveal such patient study of his material as his earlier work. He never again, except briefly in the English school life of *Bracebridge Hall* (1822), returns to the school theme. Meanwhile Cooper was busy with the romantic past in his *Leather Stocking Tales* (1823–1841), but with a past that was too much absorbed with other things to have concern for education. His Natty Bumpo thought the backwoods or the prairie no place for "book larnin'." William Gilmore Simms, who most

---

[1] Hinsdale, *Horace Mann* (N. Y., 1898), 282.

[2] D. P. Thompson, *Locke Amsden or the Schoolmaster* (Boston, 1847).

[3] Pattee, *The Development of the Short Story* (N. Y., 1923), 52.

nearly approaches Cooper in the romantic treatment of pioneer life, admits a schoolmaster into only two of his many volumes, *Beauchampe* (1842) and its sequel, *Charlemont* (1856), but in neither of the wild border tales does he take us into so tame a place as the schoolroom. The trancendentalists and their contemporaries have not yet come into their full powers. It is small wonder then that in this period of adventure and romance the school was scarcely touched, for it required a firm basis of reality. We would not expect a school story from one who was not acquainted with the interior of a schoolroom, albeit both Irving and Cooper could write of the interior of America upon only slight personal contact with it.

Nevertheless the school did get in time into the literature of the frontier and brought with it foreshadowings of the local colorists. Just as Cooper wrote of our literature as a whole in 1828 that Americans had been "tracing the outline of their great national picture" and that "the work of filling up had just commenced," so the fiction of the rural school was to follow the geographic frontier. Along with "A Romance of the Border" in THE ATLANTIC SOUVENIR for 1830 appeared the short story, *The Village School* by Richard Penn Smith; in 1833 came Warren Burton's *The District School As It Was* and Judge James Hall's *Cousin Lucy and the Village Teacher;* in 1835 *The Turn Out* and *The Debating Society* were two of Longstreet's *Georgia Scenes;* Sylvester Judd in 1845 and D. P. Thompson in 1847 in New England were paving the way for Hawthorne's more intensive use of Puritan backgrounds. In the same year (1847) James K. Paulding penned for THE BOOK OF BEAUTY ANNUAL his *Yankee Schoolmaster* frankly in the Irvingesque vein. In 1871 HEARTH AND HOME readers were laughing over the adventures of *a Hoosier School-master* and in 1864 Richard Malcolm Johnston published his realistic *Georgia Sketches* which deal extensively with plantation school life, though his work was not known to Northern readers until published in Baltimore under the title of *Dukesborough Tales* (1871). In 1879 Maurice Thompson punctured the inflated wisdom of the old backswoods pedagogue whose supposed knowledge of Latin had associated him with wizardry in the popular mind. Even as late as 1884 the April number of THE OVERLAND MONTHLY (San Francisco) carries a short story by C. T. H. Palmers entitled *A Pedagogue Primeval* which goes back to the days of '49 to tell of the beginnings of the first schools among the tents and wagons of Sacramento.

The natural arrangement of the literature dealing with the school is the topographical arrangement, for the treatment of the school is inevitably associated with the characteristic life of each frontier. Though apparently Sleepy Hollow and Flat Creek are scenes of the same activity, the district school is not the same in the East as in the West or the South. School literature in one locality may be the result of an awakened interest in education, whereas in another it may have arisen out of general indifference to education as a social function, or out of a desire to preserve a record of old times. In the latter case the literature may be the result of a feeling on the part of the author for the grotesque in life, which, as Bagehot suggests, has the value of revealing the faults of a system. School literature as a whole seems to fall into three divisions: (1) that which is a pleasant retrospect of the old days, with some effort toward historical truth; (2) that which was written out of a desire to reform the educational system; and (3) that which arises out

of a genuine interest in child life or as a "criticism of
life" in a given community. All three phases may be
present in one work, but as a rule, one predominates.
The serious interest in childhood, being a later development, does not come with the conquest of the frontiers,
but with the cultural advance that follows the wake of
the pioneers. It belongs chiefly to the cities of the East
and to cultural centers which had felt the influence of
Pestalozzian ideas.

A. NEW ENGLAND

1. THE DISTRICT SCHOOL

In New England the school can hardly be said to
figure in literature for the twenty years immediately
following Irving's memorable picture. In 1841 Hawthorne, it is true, looks back to the work of a colonial
schoolmaster of Boston in the story of Ezekiel Cheever
retold in *Grandfather's Chair* and in August, 1843 there
appeared in BOYS' AND GIRLS' MAGAZINE *Little Daffy-
downdilly*, a story of a little boy who ran away from the
cruel-visaged schoolmaster, Mr. Toil, but who, finding
the world was full of cruel schoolmasters, was glad to
return with diligence to his task. Hawthorne at least
saw the possibilities of treating the subject satirically,
for in his *American Note-Books* he placed on June 1,
1842 in juxtaposition to "Flesh and Blood"—a firm of
butchers, the solitary notation: "Miss Polly Syllable—
a schoolmistress." One book, however, does emerge in
this period which may be mentioned especially for its
historical and human value, *The District School As It
Was* by One Who Went to It. It was published first
in Boston, 1833, and was received "with unqualified
favor." The New York edition having met with success,

the work was issued in London as a book which gave "a faithful description of one of the institutions of New England."[1]   In 1850 the author got out another edition "to be disposed of to subscribers."[2]   The fact that it was issued again in 1897 with an attractive binding (Boston, Lee and Shepard) and again in 1927 (New York, Crowell) in still more attractive form is evidence of some vitality.

Of the early edition one reviewer,[3] classing it as a work of fiction, wrote: "This work . . . is as excellent in design as in the manner of its execution; and we rejoice to see it issue from the press.   It is an attempt to burlesque some of those usages against which better weapons have been directed for some time in vain.   Sure we are, that no fictitious production of the present day is more obviously calculated to be useful.   There are few persons of middle age among us who cannot bear testimony to the faithfulness with which many of the scenes are delineated.   They are scenes, however, which we hope are fast passing away."

Another reviewer writing of the mid-century edition[4] characterizes it as "an old and valuable work which has too long been out of print.   It gives a true and faithful illustration of the trials, floggings, sports and pastimes which every urchin must endure before he can become a man."   That the book was read with avidity by young and old around New England firesides is testified to by

[1] Rev. Warren Burton, *The District School As It Was*, Edited by Clifford Johnson (Boston, 1897), 6.

[2] Caroline M. Hewins in her *A Mid-century Child and Her Books* (N. Y., 1926), vividly recalls the good parson as he went about the countryside soliciting subscribers, 18.

[3] AMERICAN ANNALS OF EDUCATION (Boston, June, 1833), 288.

[4] THE WAVERLY MAGAZINE AND LITERARY REPOSITORY, a weekly magazine for ladies containing music, novels, poetry, book reviews, etc. (Boston, November 16, 1850), Vol. II, 16.

one whose memory goes back to the time.[1] Though the book has been condemned as not having literary value,[2] it must have been a relief from the dreary sentimental romances and leather-bound sermons of the period.

Near the end of the last century it was said that "the average farmer and teacher think of the rural school as a little house, on a little ground, with a little equipment, where a little teacher at a little salary, for a little while teaches little children little things."[3] Except for the grown men and women who sat on the back seats, that is essentially what the district school was a hundred years ago. Though Reverend Burton's book is expository and descriptive rather than narrative in method, it is, nevertheless, an attempt at imaginative realization of what the school was during the first quarter of the century. Memory aids him in selecting the most outstanding features: the first day and the first teacher, the spelling book and the competitions evolving from it, the first winter at school, snow-balling and other winter sports, the punishments, the exhibition, and the examination by the minister at the close of the school term. Certain teachers stand out, too, for their good or bad qualities. The name of Mary Smith, a girl of eighteen, who taught during his first summer school, has become almost a traditional symbol in American educational history for good teaching.[4] In the brief sketch of Augustus Starr, the privateer "in the late war" who turned pedagogue and whose "new crew mutinied,"

[1] Caroline Hewin, op. cit., 18. See also Barnard, AMERICAN JOURNAL OF EDUCATION, Vol. 3, 456.

[2] *Cambridge History of America Literature*, Vol. III, 418.

[3] Widely quoted saying of T. J. Coates, Late President of Eastern State Teachers College, Richmond, Ky. Died March 17, 1928.

[4] Barnard's AMERICAN JOURNAL OF EDUCATION, Vol. III, 456, 459.

the narrative becomes swift: "He knocked one lad down with his fist, hurled a stick of wood at another, which missed breaking his head because it struck the ceiling, making a dent which fearfully indicated what would have been the consequences had the skull been hit."[1]   Again in the narrative of the exhibition and of Mr. Spoutsound, the speaking master, who was a very lion at roaring, the author reveals a sense of humor as well as a sense of fact. Great preparation had been made both at home and at school for the occasion.   The crowd packed into the small room to the sound of the bass viol and clarionet.   "At forty five minutes past six, the curtains rose; that is, the bed blankets were pulled aside.   There stood Mr. Spoutsound on the stage, in all the pomp possible to diminutiveness."   His   utterance   seemed   a   "vocal cataract, all torrent, thunder, froth.   But it wanted room—an abyss to empty into.   A few of the audience were overwhelmed with the pour and rush and roar of pent up noise, and the rest with admiration, yea, astonishment that a schoolmaster 'could speak so!' "[2]   But all this happened in "the district school *as it was*, not as it should be."   After this school Mr. Spoutsound migrated to the States beyond the Allegheny where it was rumored that "he soon spoke himself into the legislature."[3]

The books used in the school as it was were: *The Only Sure Guide to the English Tongue* by William Perry, Lecturer of the English Language in the Academy of Edinburgh, Murray's *Young Lady's Accidence* in which little boys were set to parsing (pronounced passing), at the age of seven, Pope's *Essay on Man* as the parsing

[1] Ibid., 116.
[2] Ibid., 75.
[3] Ibid., 77.

manual for the most advanced, Scott's *Lessons in Reading*, Adam's *Understanding Reader*, and Adam's *Arithmetic* followed by "old Pike." This last subject was the "chiefest of sciences in Yankee estimation." Near the end of Burton's experience, composition was introduced by one of the young college students who taught the winter school, but this belonged to the school "as it should be." At the exhibition the children spoke patriotic pieces from the *American Preceptor*, the *Columbian Orator*, the *Art of Reading*, *Scott's Elocution* and *Webster's Third Part*.[1]

The methods of punishment used were feruling on the palm of the hand, whipping on the back with a rod, standing with a book held out at arm's length or in a stooping posture with the finger on the head of a nail in the floor (sometimes directly in front of an enormous fire); inserting a chip perpendicularly between the teeth as an antidote for whispering, pulling the hair, tweaking the nose, pinching or boxing the ears, and, worst of all, making little boys sit in the girls' seats or *vice versa*. Punishment, which in the frontier school was a relic of older and more severe discipline, was a chief interest factor to children. Learning, it was thought, was probable more likely to take place through annoyance than through satisfaction. The doctrine of original sin and depravity of children lingered in America as long as there was a frontier.[2] The rod of correction must drive out the foolishness that is bound up in the heart of a child. Parents believed in rigorous discipline, for both the Old Testament and the ministry would not allow them to forget it. Their own lives were severe and their children must be taught to work. "Work hard whether

[1] Ibid., 68.
[2] James Michel Williams, *Our Rural Heritage* (Knopf, 1925).

you learn anything or not" and "what you need is to learn to apply yourself" were slogans in the homes of the *school as it was.*[1] The sons of Revolutionary fighters were not a people to molly-coddle their children, but they were men who believed in "no excellence without labor."[2]

So great was this belief in individual exertion and industry that the kind of teacher or school, it seems, were not matters of prime importance. If the sons were to become farmers and the daughters, farmers' wives, the school existed simply to augment what was learned on the farm and in the home.[3] It was this attitude, no doubt, which was a factor in making them content with the decaying district system of the early half of the century.

Again the general attitude of parents toward their children was that of authority. Children must be made to "mind;" the word "why" would not be tolerated, for parents assumed authority beyond question. Children must not only be made to conform to their parents' wishes, but they must be moulded into the beliefs and customs of the neighborhood.[4] Parents were, therefore, often grateful when their children were corrected at school. They themselves had been accustomed to discipline at school and looked back upon the custom with approval. The schoolmaster, who before the days of dissent in New England shared fully in the beliefs and customs of the community, usually got parental support in the administration of discipline, though Eggleston

[1] Williams, Ibid., 36.

[2] James Wirt in *McGuffey's Fourth Reader* (Cincinnati, 1837), 48.

[3] Thompson, *Locke Amsden* (Boston, 1890), 16.

[4] Williams, op. cit., 158.

Johnson, op. cit., 78, 79.

records that on the western frontier parents often took pride in the initiative of children in attacking the teacher.[1] As religious dissent spread, the master often found himself in communities where he had to play the delicate rôle of non-sectarian; the friction in the community meant trouble in the school.[2]

That pioneer children were pugnacious and unruly in spite of the strict disciplinary measures in home and school is abundantly borne out by fiction and autobiography. The active life on the frontier, the large families, the convocation of old and young, male and female pupils into one school, gave plenty of stimulus to quarreling.[3] On the other hand, since muscular strength and prowess had high value in pioneer communities, the large boys were not slow to test these qualities both in themselves and the teacher. It was the large boys who led the mutiny in Augustus Starr's crew which hurled the luckless pedagogue over an embankment into bramble bushes where he was never seen more.[4] One account tells of a schoolmaster whose head was thrust by force into the stove, his eyebrows and eyelashes singed off, his eyesight ruined for life, and his health injured by the violence of the older boys.[5] Another account relates how the pupils' unruliness was overawed only by the use of an empty revolver.[6] The Hoosier

[1] Eggleston, *The Hoosier Schoolmaster* (N. Y., 1899), 146.

[2] NOTE: One case is recorded where a teacher was tabooed because he, being ignorant of the custom the people had at church of standing reverently in their places until the minister had walked down the aisle, had proceeded first. Burton, op. cit., 120.

[3] Williams, op. cit., 156.

[4] Burton, op. cit., Chap. XVIII.

[5] THE COMMON SCHOOL JOURNAL (Boston, 1847), Vol. IV, 325.

[6] Nelson, "The Little Red Schoolhouse" (in Maine, 1856–59), EDUCATIONAL REVIEW, Vol. 23, 304–17.

Schoolmaster was, doubtless, saved from a like violence by a tactful cultivation of the friendship of one of the strongest.

The large boy as a rule never looked beyond the district school to the high school, as does his younger country cousin of today; hence there was not the same incentive to study. The reliance of the rural people on oral tradition made them think of memorization as a synonym for education.[1] What a child could "recite" was proof of what he had learned at school, no matter how uninteresting the facts were. Under this condition compulsion was often necessary; but older boys would often rather fight or be expelled than memorize *Cardinal Wolsey's Farewell*. As a result up to 1875, fights and the use of the rod are major activities in nearly all stories of the district school life. Here at least is food for romance of the piratical order.

If before the middle of the century the birch had attained a place in American life and literature hardly equalled by any other tree,[2] a reaction set in during the common school revival for the ultimate overthrow of coercion. After the Civil War attacks upon the "shallow theorist who hold out for flogging" in schools had become prominent in educational journals. "If present public opinion regards the flogging of negroes as barbarous, why should it not so regard the flogging of pupils".[3] The argument against flogging was that it inevitably caused a hatred for the teacher and this in turn engendered a dislike for study. Hence whipping defeats its purpose. "In the schoolroom the teacher is an absolute monarch,

[1] Williams, op. cit., 156–58.

Johnston, *Dukesborough Tales* (Baltimore, 1871), 14, 20.

[2] Barnard's AMERICAN JOURNAL OF EDUCATION, Vol. 28, 851.

[3] THE AMERICAN EDUCATIONAL MONTHLY (Jan., 1867), 36. (Feb. 1867), 67.

and absolute monarchy with offences to the monarch leads to abuse." He was the offended party, police, witness, lawyer, jury, judge, and sheriff all in one and these seven offices being filled in too rapid succession, mere passionate blundering was often the result.[1] But there was some consolation in the fact that if he was like the Czar, "he was despised out of his dominion and was regarded as an old map of some barren island."[2]

That there was in New England little treatment of the school in imaginative literature during the second quarter of the century is hardly more than would be expected. The vigorous old district system, which had adequately met the needs of the colonists, had by this time proved pitifully insufficient. Under this system the great body of the people in Massachusetts had become lethargic to the larger educational needs that were inevitably ushered in by the development of the new industrialism and by the social changes that came with the growth of the cities. "On its secluded little farms New England had lived a narrow parochial life, cooping up its mind in a rigid theological system, and disciplining its character by a self-denying ordinance."[3] If aroused at all in educational matters, it was over some petty detail in a native districts—a new chimney or how cheaply the next schoolmaster might be employed. So great had this decline become by 1826 that the district schools might well be referred to as "cemeteries of eddication."[4]

---

[1] Ibid. (Oct., 1866), 381.

[2] THE AMERICAN MUSEUM, Vol. III, 147.

[3] Parrington, *Main Currents in American Thought*, Vol. II, 273.

[4] "Horace Mann and the Revival of Education in Massachusetts," by George H. Martin, EDUCATIONAL REVIEW, Vol. V, 434–450.

Moreover, if the intellectual and literary renaissances in New England as a part of the great European liberal movements were tardy in appearing, the educational renaissance was still more tardy. The seed sown by a Channing on the barren soil of a decadent Calvinism must take root before Horace Mann, the Unitarian, could begin his work of the secularization of education.[1] Emerson has pointedly expressed the utter sterility of the time when he wrote in his Journals:[2] "To write a history of Massachusetts, I confess, is not inviting to an expansive thinker. . . . From 1790 to 1820 there was not a book, a speech, a conversation, or a thought in the state. About 1820, the Channing, Webster, and Everett era begun, and we have been bookish and poetical and cogitative ever since." But other forces were at work besides Unitarianism and oratory. France, Germany, and England all had a part in the literary and educational awakening in New England—an awakening whose deep romantic purpose was "to humanize the emerging society, to [arouse] it to a nobler faith in human destiny, to further the cause of social justice and to create a democracy of the spirit."[3]

Who knows what part the liberalizing spirit of Franklin may have had in this new educational movement, for it was in a town which changed its name to Franklin and which received a library at the hands of this founder of the Republic that Horace Mann grew up! It was later largely through Mann's efforts that a revival of town

[1] In 1805 the Hollis Professorship of Divinity was given to Rev. Henry Ware, an avowed Unitarian. Wendel, *History of Literature in America*, 233. In 1819 Channing preached his famous sermon in Baltimore.

[2] Emerson, *Works* Vol. VIII, 339.

[3] Parrington, op. cit., Vol. II, 319.

libraries spread through his state.[1] Though he was not
the first to point out the decadent condition of the
public schools in Massachusetts,[2] his was the chief voice
crying in the wilderness. The weight of his reports as
Secretary of the Massachusetts Board of Education
(1837–1848), of his lectures and addresses and of his
trenchant and vigorous pen was felt throughout all the
Northern States. Through the annual conventions held
in each county of his state he brought such eloquence and
zeal, such logic and energy of diction, and such a musical
voice and graceful manner that his audience was usually
captivated.[3] His demands were for more rational and
humane methods in governing children, for the introduction of an enriched curriculum, for the training of teachers, for the adoption of methods based on a scientific
knowledge of the human mind, and for "elaboration of
the public school system to include many if not all of the
quasi-public organizations so numerous in America."[4]
That these demands should arouse controversy with the
old authorities of the "tie-wig school," who were tena-
cious of the rights of the district system and of the private
and church schools, was unavoidable. The debate got
into the newspapers and magazines, and grew to national
proportions. Though Barnard and many others worked
with no less energy than Horace Mann, it was Mann's
good fortune, since the factors necessary to a great
educational reform were brought into harmony when he

[1] Bassett, *A Short History of the United States* (N. Y., 1920), 476.
[2] Hinsdale, op. cit., *Forerunners of Horace Mann*, Chap. II,
43–75.
[3] Duyckinck, Vol. II, 224; Martin, op. cit., EDUCATIONAL
REVIEW, Vol. V, 440.
[4] *Cambridge History of American Literature*, Vol. III, 408.
Hinsdale, op. cit., 272–275.

began his work, to have his name most generally connected with the movement.[1]

Another factor influencing the returning interest in the schoolmaster and his work as literary material may have been the popularity of Dickens in America. The year before his first visit to this country, Horace Greeley had given a column on the front page of the NEW YORK TRIBUNE for a serial run of *Barnaby Rudge* (May 1 to July 10, 1841). Even before Dickens' arrival, his American audience must have been acquainted with his sympathy for unfortunate children in *Oliver Twist* (1837); with the kindly Mr. Martin of the *Old Curiosity Shop* (1840); and of his attack upon the brutal coercion of Squeers at Dotheboys Hall (*Nicholas Nichleby*, 1838). In his first work at the age of twenty-two Dickens had revealed an interest in child life at school (Minerva House in *Sketches of Boz*, 1835). By the middle of the century he was to become the first great English student of the kindergarten and to make known his interest in Froebel and his work in an article for HOUSEHOLD WORDS (1853).[2] By this time also both English and American readers were to know his satire upon the various forms of cramming in Doctor Blimber's and the Grinder's schools (*Dombey* and *Son*, 1846) and upon the memorization of meaningless facts to the exclusion of the culture of the imagination in Mr. McChoakkumchild's school.[3] In the year just before his first American visit and during the interval of twenty-five years between his two visits to the United States Dickens dealt with twenty-eight schools in his writings in addition to his brief sketches of real schools in his *American Notes*

[1] Hinsdale, op. cit., 271.

[2] Hughes, *Dickens as an Educator* (N. Y., 1900), 3, 14–29.

[3] *Hard Times* (1854). Hughes, op. cit., 136–162.

(1842).[1] Such an interest in child life and education has caused one student of Dickens to say that he was consciously and intentionally an educator.[2] At any rate he revealed the possibilities of the realistic novel as a means of awakening educational interest.

This was just the purpose of the first novel in America to choose the school as the center of its action—*Locke Amsden or The Schoolmaster* (1847) by Daniel Pierce Thompson, now almost forgotten. It is here that the old district school and its master get their fullest literary presentation. *The Legend of Sleepy Hollow* throws them upon the screen for a moment, distinctly and clearly, but in caricature. If Irving had chosen to sketch Ichabod at his next destination, he might have done so with less superstitious circumstances. But the novel was not Irving's forte, and we shall not quarrel with him for what he did in making a legend of the school-master's craft. His purpose was not reform, but mellow laughter; and he succeeded well.

Locke Amsden, on the other hand, appearing as it did in the light of the work of Mann and Barnard, and dedicated to the friends of popular education, was written not so much "with the hope of gaining literary fame" as "of awakening an interest and imparting useful hints on an important, and, with all our boasts, a *still* sadly neglected subject." The book was therefore too much a novel with a purpose, too realistic, not sufficiently florid, to call forth comment from the reviewers of the LITERARY REPOSITORY and the GODEY LADY'S BOOK, who thought that fiction should deal with a refined and

[1] After attending a Temperance Convention in Cincinnati, he visited classrooms of public schools, Chap. XI; he was interested in the life at West Point, Chap. XV.

[2] Hughes, op. cit., 1.

idealized society. But in the leading article of the COMMON SCHOOL JOURNAL of Horace Mann for the month of November, 1847,[1] Thompson's illustration of common school principles through the medium of fiction is enthusiastically hailed as something new. "Here is a regular-built novel, love story and all,—the hero of which is a country common schoolmaster. The scene is professedly laid in the 'northern portion of the union', but all attendant circumstances limit it to the meridian of New England. The main action of the piece is the keeping of two country schools; but the incidents connected with these furnish the occasions for setting forth all the mischief of bad schools and all the blessings of good ones . . . For the first time this neglected and often times despised theme is brought within the domain of popular literature. It is ornamented by the skill of an easy writer, and dignified by the reflections of a sound thinker. The schoolmaster is introduced for the purpose of being honored and not ridiculed; and yet neither Irving nor Dickens who have often portrayed the incompetent, but never recognized the possibilities of the competent common schoolmaster;—neither has written anything which reflects such deserved odium upon incompetency as this book. It debases the low by exalting the excellent; it shows in a most truthful manner how a good district school will in the course of a few years, entirely renovate the character of a neighborhood."[2]

Coming thus during the awakening interest in education and in the midst of the battle for the control of education between the forces of public and private schools, the book gives expression to many ideas of the

[1] *Locke Amsden: or the Schoolmaster a Tale.* THE COMMON SCHOOL JOURNAL, Vol. IX, 320, 332.

[2] Ibid., 321, 330.

reformers. The general ignorance of the schoolmaster[1] together with even worse stupidity, prejudice, and superstition on the part of the school committeemen,[2] the low estimation in which the occupation of the common teacher is held by the public[3] as well as the small interest that country people have in learning,[4] the badly constructed schoolhouses with their poor ventilation,[5] torturing seats, and crude furniture;[6] the brutal discipline of the time together with the conflict of master and pupil,[7] the sadly defective condition of the common schools as a whole, and the shallow Chesterfieldianism of the village aristocracy which demands a select school for its children to the disadvantage of the common school[8] —all these abuses come in for the butt of his keen but sane ridicule. But these defects, he maintains, can be remedied by the power of a competent teacher—a teacher who is far-seeing enough to know that reform must begin in the community as well as in the school. "I tell you we have got to raise the qualifications of the trustees as well as the teachers," declares Doctor Lincoln, the friend of education.[9] In the matter of discipline the teacher and parent must coöperate; whipping, if necessary, should take place in the presence of the parent. Certainly a teacher who is keenly alive to learning will have little trouble in arousing sufficient interest to reduce

[1] Thompson, op. cit., 18, 31.

[2] Ibid., 51–57.

Ibid., "pitiful ignoramuses," 96–122; 140–143, 144–146, 147.

[3] Ibid., 180.

[4] Ibid., 177.

[5] Ibid., 98, 107–119.

[6] Ibid., 54.

[7] Ibid., 57–60, 93.

[8] Ibid., 184–189.

[9] Ibid., 47.

discipline to a minimum.[1]   The natural sciences should
be an aid in arousing this interest, and the teacher
should be alive to material surrounding him in the country and to the need of more scientific farming.[2]

It is easy to see that the book involves no inconsider-
able part of the author's own experiences in a pioneer
community.   Born in Charleston, Massachusetts, in
1795, where his father had been unsuccessful in business,
he came along with the family in 1800 to a wild farm
remote from schools and churches in the town of Berlin,
Vermont, not far from present-day Montpelier.[3]   The only
school in the town in 1789 was in a log building, but in
the winter of 1791–2 the school was moved for greater
comfort into the new frame house of Colonel Davis.
By 1794 the population of the community had increased
to such an extent that the town was divided into six
districts, and schools were shortly established in all of
them.   On November 7, 1800 "The Trustees of the
Montpelier Academy" were incorporated and in October,
1813, an act of the legislature changed[4] the academy into
a county institution,[5] appropriating rents of the grammar
school lands lying within the county.   The youth grew
up to farm labor such as is vividly described in the story,
and made scanty attendance at the district school.   But
as Thompson's mother was a descendent of Ezekiel
Cheever it was natural that there should be some
hereditary pull toward education.   The good judge

[1] Ibid., 88.

[2] Ibid., 17, 127.

[3] Duyckinck, op. cit., 215; John S. Hart, *A Manual of American
Literature* (Philadelphia, 1873); *The American Cyclopedia.*

[4] D. P. Thompson, *History of Montpelier* (Montpelier, 1860),
87–89.

[5] Ibid., 94–96.

represents this in his story as all coming from the side of the mother.[1] It was she who intercedes with the father to grant the boy leave from the farm to go to the academy, and yet she holds education light "as compared with the things of heaven." The scarcity of books in these pioneer homes[2] is no barrier to this zeal to know, for thorough use is made of those which come by chance. When Thompson was sixteen a spring flood brought down a muddied volume of poetry from which for the first time he eagerly read verses from the English poets— Pope, Goldsmith, and Cowper, who became the schoolmaster's favorites. In the story, the books came as a surprise gift from a chance visitor. In the story, also, the boy's learning from the land surveyor in the town,[3] the electioneering for a better qualified schoolmaster, the boy's diligence on the farm as a means to education, the school-keeping at fourteen dollars a month and board, the entrance into college with advanced standing,[4] and the ultimate political success, all seem to have a basis in the facts of the author's life. Even the minor incidents of school life, though apparently exaggerated, seem to have foundation in personal observation.[5]

Though the story may deal largely with an individual experience, it is, nevertheless, peculiarly adapted to New England. Note how this foreshadows the era of localized romance: A boy possessing high endowments with a zeal to know, the passion for self-education, the belief in thoroughness; Bunker, the blacksmith's belief that

[1] *Locke Amsden*, 45–46.
[2] Ibid., 81.
[3] Ibid., 36.
[4] Ibid., 125–126.
[5] *Locke Amsden*, op. cit., author's footnote, 99.

education is a training to think as well as his insistence upon thoroughness in "this reading and surface-skimming age,"[1] his illiterate method of bookkeeping which could confuse a cheese and a grindstone, yet his inborn common sense which prided itself on solving problems independently; the boylife in sugar camps, the hospitality to refined strangers, the lingering beliefs among the ignorant of "Woollen Marther's" *black art;* and, near the end of the story, the flourishing villages with their large proportion of attractive dwellings and an accompanying aristocracy. Speaking for the people of his state at the unveiling of the tablet inscription in the State Capitol, January 19, 1915, Governor Bailey said: "Judge Thompson did more to hand down and perpetuate the early history of Vermont than any other person living or dead. . . . He has woven into an enchanting story the great drama of the first fifty years of our existence."[2] Though his *Green Mountain Boys* and *May Martin* had exceeded fifty editions by 1860,[3] *Locke Amsden* is a more faithful record of the pioneer life of the state than his other work.

The plot of the story is accidental and chronological, concerning itself chiefly with the progress, development and experiences of a single character. Some attempt is made to weave a subordinated love romance into it, but

[1] Ibid., 74.

[2] Proceedings of the Vermont Historical Society, 1913–15, 302.

NOTE: The inscription is: "This tablet erected by the state of Vermont to the honored memory of Daniel Pierce Thompson, Author, Editor, Lawyer, Judge, Secretary of State." Then follow the place and date of birth and death together with a list of his published works.

[3] Thompson's *History of Montpelier*, op. cit., 163.

the author suggestively kept love out of his story until after the close of his hero's second year of successful teaching at Cartersville, where he scored a victory over the master of the Select Academy of Elegant Literature. He is not so much at home in describing the "tender passion" as in narrating the examination by school committeemen. These village types come out in the story as the tailor, the editor, the doctor, and the blacksmith, only to advance or retard the schoolmaster's career. The trial, which was an almost always unavoidable concomitant of frontier school life, is introduced and brings with it an element of suspense. In an undeveloped subplot the conventional elopement of one of the daughters of aristocracy with the master of the select academy is interpolated—a plot frequently found in English boarding school dramas.[1] The novel ends with a fire from which the hero schoolmaster rescues the charming Mary; then he is nursed back to health like a Lancelot. The long lost father of Mary returns bringing back an immense fortune. He gives his consent to their marriage, and Cartersville now has a new school building through the munificence of Mr. Amsden, Member of Congress. Here is a romance if ever schoolmaster knew it; but, though humorous, it is very poorly narrated. In this last romantic scene the judge could not avoid the florid style of his contemporaries, and his novel loses much of its honest realism. But his purpose was not to write a romance; he simply threw that in extra to show that school teachers are human and that, if successful

---

[1] Charles Coffey, *The Boarding School* (London, 1733).

W. B. Bernard, *The Boarding School* (London, 1841), cf. John Howard Payne, *The Boarding School*, performed Park Theatre (N. Y., 1841).

in their vocation, they may succeed in matrimony, wealth, and fame.[1]

2. ACADEMIES AND BOARDING SCHOOLS

The district school of New England finds expression in the child literature of the time, but that has been reserved for later treatment. Child life at school does not seem to have occurred to Thompson, bent as he was upon reform and a truthful record of the schoolmaster's experiences. Boarding schools and academies for boys and girls, however, appeared in the literature of New England during the same period. But the literature of the boarding school belongs to the culture of the towns in the older communities—not to the frontier of the district school. In the second quarter of the century the rapid increase in the number of academies was as marked as the development of the public schools. In 1820 Massachusetts numbered thirty-six such institutions, but by 1850 the number was increased to four hundred three, while in the whole of New England according to Inglis[2] there were not less than one thousand seven. This rapid increase is reflected in the newspaper advertisements of the time. For the month of October, 1841, the NEW YORK TRIBUNE presented never more than ten such notices, while thirty years later it carried ten times that number. Typical entries were: Grammar and Boarding Schools for Girls, Rural Home School for Girls, Military Boarding School, A Home School for Boys, Family School for Girls, and Dancing Academy. It

[1] Cf. the treatment of love-theme in *The Country Schoolmaster in Love or Life in New England*—A College Poem by Rev. James Cook Richmond (N. Y., 1845).

[2] Cited in Cubberley, *Public Education in the United States*, 185.

being thought from early colonial days that intellectual accomplishments were out of the question for women, a special kind of education had been provided for them in the private school.[1] Even during the middle of the nineteenth century, it was popular for the children of the upper class to attend boarding school. "There was no thought of sending me to a public school," wrote E. E. Hale.[2]

In 1821 Timothy Dwight[3] had spoken out against this "type of education which is chiefly confined to people of fashion" whose aim was "to make their children objects of admiration." To this end such light subjects as music, dancing, embroidery, ease, confidence, gracefulness, manners, reading, and traveling were taught so that children might "mingle without awkwardness into that empty, unmeaning chat" which is the mere vibration of the tongue known as fashionable conversation. Such a school was the Select Female Academy of *Locke Amsden*, and it is to such a school, the Apollinean Female Institute, that Holmes sends his pre-natally poisoned Elsie Venner for the testing out and the revelation of the effects of her malady—the natural place to try feminine frailties to the breaking point. He had given a humorous treatment of such a school in "My Aunt" as early as 1831:[4]

> He sent her to a stylish school
> 'Twas in her thirteenth June
> And with her, as the rules required
> Two towels and a spoon.

[1] Andrews, *Colonial Folkways* (Yale, 1921), 143–144.
[2] *A New England Boyhood* (Boston, 1893), 23.
[3] *Travels*, op. cit., Vol. I, 512, 519.
[4] NEW ENGLAND MAGAZINE (October, 1831).

> They braced my aunt against a board,
> To make her straight and tall;
> They laced her up, they starved her down,
> To make her light and small.
>
> They pinched her feet, they singed her hair,
> They screwed it up with pins;
> Oh, never mortal suffered more
> In penance for her sins.
>
> So when my precious aunt was done,
> My grandsire brought her back
> By daylight, lest some rabid youth
> Might follow on the track.

"Every girl ought to walk locked close, arm in arm, between two guardian angels," cries Helen Darley, the "Miss Polly Syllable" of *Elsie Venner*. "Alas! It is a dreadful thing to have charge of their souls and bodies."[1]

The typical schoolmistress of fiction, says R. M. Whitney in an address in Brooklyn, 1874[2] is a "lady of twenty to fifty years of age, tall, not by any means ill-looking, who wears convex glasses . . . and thrusts pluperfect participles and isosceles triangles down your throat on slightest provocation. If she ever had a lover, she amazed him to the borders of epilepsy by requiring him, on first visit, as a prelude to marital intimations, to parse some of the longest sentences in *Paradise Lost*. If he has the hardihood to offer his heart, she replies: 'Cannot you contrive, sir, to make your verbs agree with their nominatives in number and person?'" Helen Darley of the Apollinean Female Institute is not such a

---

[1] Holmes, *Elsie Venner* (Boston, 1861), 73.

[2] Whitney, *The Schoolmistress in History, Poetry, and Romance —An Address* (Brooklyn, 1874), 2, 3.

schoolmistress, though she might easily have so developed. The drilling in hard facts has not squeezed out quite all the warm blood in her veins.   Conscientious, meticulous, and transcendental she may be, but underneath all she reveals the true woman in her almost chivalrous loyalty to her strange and brilliant pupil.

The story *Elsie Venner* began serially in the ATLANTIC MONTHLY December, 1859, under the title of *The Professor's Story*.[1] When it appeared in book form two years later, it was dedicated to "the schoolmistress who has furnished some outlines made use of in these pages . . . by her oldest scholar."   It relates the experiences of a young medical student, Barnard Langdon, who found it necessary to teach for a year before being able to finish his course.   This was how the Professor came to tell of the interesting "case" of one of the pupils in the Female Institute.

It was in giving the family backgrounds of the young schoolmaster that Holmes defined the Brahmin of New England.[2]   Prominent on college rolls, the son of a scholarly ancestry, he is apt to be pallid; his face is smooth, the features regular and delicate, "his eyes bright and quick,—his lips play over the thought he utters as a pianist's fingers dance over music,—and his whole air, though it may be timid, and even awkward, has nothing clownish."   If you are his teacher you will see that he "will take to his books as a pointer or a setter to his field work."   If Holmes seems a little unfair to the country-bred boy of the type of Locke Amsden, it is because he is quoting the rule and not the exception.

[1] Holmes had already written *The Autocrat of the Breakfast Table and The Professor*.

[2] Ibid., 2–4.

Young Langdon, before being invited to the Institute, first kept a country school at Pigwacket Center District No. 1, where he subdued the proverbial big boy, being thrice armed with Brahminism, and drove him and his vicious cur from the school. The chapter dealing with the schoolhouse—grim, old, and red—perched on a bare rock at the top of a hill, its unpainted desks brown with the umber of human contact and hacked with innumerable jack-knives, its civil wars of papier-mâché missiles, approaches Irving's vividness and humor. It is as if Holmes said: "Young Brahmins have no business meddling in such vulgar business as a district school; female institutes are more appropriate." All the main characters of the story, except Dick Venner and Old Sophy, are connected in one way or another with the Institute: Elsie, Mr. Peckham, Mr. Langdon, Helen Darley, who feels strange influences from Elsie, and Mr. Venner, a trustee. Silas Peckham, the keeper of this "first-class establishment" was one of those dealers in morality who advertise religious goods and character building to credulous parents. He had a thick nasal twang "which not rarely becomes hereditary after three or four generations raised upon east winds, salt fish, and large white-bellied, pickled cucumbers." He kept a school exactly as he would have kept a hundred head of cattle—for the simple, unadorned purpose of making just as much money in just as few years as could safely be done. Not concerned much with the department of instruction, he was always busy with contracts for flour and potatoes, beef, pork and other staples. "The real business of the school was making money by taking young girls in as boarders."[1] In Mrs. Peckham, we have the first notable portrait in American literature of the schoolmaster's wife.

[1] Ibid., 34, 35.

From the West, "raised on Indian corn and pork," a little coarse-fibred, she specialized in looking after "the feathering, cackling, roosting, rising and general behavior of the hundred chicks. An honest, ignorant woman, she could not have passed an examination in the youngest class."[1]

On account of his mean and grasping method of grinding the life out of his teachers, it was old Peckham who roused the youthful blood of Barnard Langdon. With what irony Holmes makes the old miser say to Helen Darley whose efforts had kept the school flourishing—and this just when he has cut her quarterly wages from seventy-five dollars to thirty-two dollars and six cents because she was absent a few days to comfort the dying Elsie—"Women's wages can't be expected to do more than clothe and feed 'em, as a gineral thing, with a little savin', in case of sickness, and to bury 'em, if they break down, as all of 'em are like to do at any time."[2] To give us a picture of the drudgery of Helen before Mr. Barnard came, Holmes allows us to see her with a bundle of themes on her table. Though she has already performed a full day's work, "she was conscientious in her duties, and would insist on reading every sentence,—there was no saying where she might find faults of grammar or bad spelling;" this, too, in spite of the fact that she already knew the leading sentiments they contained: "that beauty was subject to the accidents of time; that wealth was inconstant, and existence uncertain; that virtue is its own reward; that life was overshadowed with trials; that the lessons of virtue instilled by our beloved teachers were to be our guides through all our future career." The imagery employed consisted principally

[1] Ibid., 35.
[2] Ibid., 349, 350.

of roses, lilies, birds, clouds, and brooks, with the celebrated comparison of a wayward genius to a meteor.
But drudgery was rewarded when, getting sleepy in spite
of herself, she came upon the theme of her unique pupil
which startled her.[1]

Early critics dealt with the book severely, some refer-
ring to it as the snake story of literature par excellence
but objecting to such doctrines of ante-natal influence as
being "inartistic;"[2] others saying that a novel with a
purpose rarely survives the elimination of the purpose
from the popular interest.[3] Later critics regard it as
being brilliantly conversational and discursive, resem-
bling more closely the author's earlier work than the
great models of fiction in England.[4] Neither, however,
can deny that local color was never sketched with more
shrewdness than in such vignettes as the school in District No. 1, the Appollinean Institute, and the party at
"the elegant residence of our distinguished citizen, Colonel Sprowle." The caste system, the mansion, houses,
the variety of school girls and their compositions,
the two clergymen of the village—one Liberal and the
other Calvinist each covertly leaning to the other's
faith—the old India merchant, the oysters, the hired
help, the colonial chimneys, and the hemlock trees leave
us in no doubt as to where the story has its setting.
Moreover, to modern educators interested in case studies
Elsie Venner should be of perpetual interest.

[1] Ibid., 51–52, 123–124.

[2] Living Age, Vol. 71, 435–443.

J. T. Morse, Jr., *Life and Letters of Oliver Wendell Holmes*
(London, 1896), Vol. I, 258, 265.

[3] Ibid., 256–257.

[4] *Cambridge History of American Literature*, op. cit., Vol. II, 228.
Pattee, *History of American Literature Since* 1870 (N. Y., 1915),
63–65.

The decade from 1860 to 1870 was a lean period in American fictional history;[1] but during these years Louisa M. Alcott was making ready to present her memorable portraits of child life in her *Little Women* and its sequel (1868). Aldrich, *The Story of a Bad Boy* (1869) and Trowbridge, *Cudjo's Cave* (1864) were, too, bringing a new realism into literature for children. By 1873 two extended stories of New England life were written, *Arthur Bonnicastle* (Holland, N. Y., 1873) and *Antony Brade*,[2] both of which, though falling far short in literary quality, resemble Hughes' *Tom Brown's School Days* (1857) in purpose. Selections from Hughes' famous story had been quickly placed in American school readers . . . especially the incident where Tom exhibits moral courage in saying his prayers.[3] In 1870 Hughes visited America without "condescension" and was almost as enthusiastically received in the cities as Dickens. Lowell looked upon him as being a pledge of friendship between England and America.[4] At any rate his *Dare to Do Right*, no doubt, became the father of many school stories in America and, if we may trust a contemporary historian, it profoundly influenced American leadership.[5]

Antony Brade, lovingly written for boys and dedicated to "all who have been boys or are boys or like boys," gives pictures of life at a boy's school under Episcopal influences . . . St. Mark's School for Boys. It might be referred to as an English public school transplanted to a New England country town. The plot centers

---

[1] Whitcomb, op. cit., 176–187.

[2] Robert T. S. Lowell (Boston, 1873).

[3] NOTE: McGuffey places this scene in his *Revised Fourth Reader* under the title of "Dare to Do Right." See also *A Rhetorical Reader* by Robert Kidd (Cincinnati and N. Y., 1870), 315, 321.

[4] See Lowell's *Letters to Thomas Hughes*, October, 18, 1870.

[5] Mark Sullivan, *Our Times* (N. Y., 1927), Vol. II, 39.

around the mystery of Antony Brade, a student, who has not revealed his identity to anyone apparently. This furnishes the source of much gossip in the little village which reaches the height of farcical ridicule when, after the story that the boy is a Russian of royal lineage, a Russian dinner is given in his honor and the Russian ambassador informed of his distinguished countryman. Antony and his cousin, Miss Ryan, in circulating this story were testing the gullibility of village gossips to the extreme. In this huge prank as well as in his studies, his scheming, and his play with his companions, Antony is a thoroughly boy-like figure.

Trapping for game at school, though a digression, is a lively chapter. It makes the story realistic by leading to some brutal fighting, which, in turn, gives the kindly rector an opportunity to draw the appropriate lesson that fighting is not Christian. "We excuse wars, because nations make their people go into them; but they should have been done away with eighteen hundred years ago." There is no hint of flogging in the entire volume.

The story evidently reflects Robert Lowell's experiences as headmaster of St. Mark's School for Boys, Southboro, Massachusetts (1869–73). The dilatory, sleepy, meddlesome, yet inactive trustees; the board meeting with its hint of financial difficulties; the sympathetic headmaster who knew boys well enough not to meddle too much in their affairs, or to wish to find out all he could of their activities; the gossiping village women— all these make the story as true of New England and of the boys' boarding school as *Elsie Venner* is of the girls' school.

Though the school is romantically treated, the narrative as a whole moves too slowly, lacks focus, and is interrupted by too many digressions. It missed a possible appeal to the mature because of its limited scope, and to the young because of its heaviness. Accounts of secret societies, trustees, board meetings, benefactor's day, and even boyish pranks do not make lively reading. Robert Lowell, three years older than his brother, James Russell, nevertheless, had a distinct literary gift.[1] He is better known by his poem "The Relief of Lucknow," which James Russell Lowell published in THE ATLANTIC during his editorship.

It was Robert who, after the death of Josiah Gilbert Holland, wrote an appreciation of his friend's writings, including his school story, *Arthur Bonnicastle*.[2] Later he published an article telling how Mr. Holland found his schoolmaster in the character of a bachelor clergyman of Adrian, Michigan.[3] Be that as it may, many who read the twelve installments of Holland's novel[4] recognized in the Birds' Nest the well-known "Gunnery" school of Washington, Connecticut, which was attended by the sons of such ardent abolitionists as H. W. Beecher, Mrs. Stowe, and John C. Fremont. It was conducted by the justly famous Frederick William Gunn (1816– 1881) and his wife whose system of discipline and family meetings on Sunday evening in which the boys give an account of their misdemeanors during the week, are exactly those of Father and Mother Bird in *Arthur Bonnicastle*.[5] Mr. Gunn's believed in two principles: (1) that "a boy must learn to do the right, to love it, and to dare to defend it" and (2) "if you would get into a boy's heart, you must get the boy's heart into you."

[1] Horace E. Scudder, *James Russell Lowell* (Boston, 1901), 41.

[2] NORTH AMERICAN REVIEW, Vol. 95, 122–132.

[3] EDUCATION, Vol. XII (May, 1892), 545–6.

[4] SCRIBNER'S MAGAZINE, Nov., 1872 to Nov., 1873.

[5] *National Encyclopedia of American Biography*, Vol. XIII, 349. *Arthur Bonnicastle*, op. cit., 71, 72, 77, 88.

He was a companion to the boys in school, at games, and on excursions. "Confidence was met with confidence and their affection for him was as profound as their respect."[1]   These were the principles and *modus operandi* of Mr. Bird of *Arthur Bonnicastle*. Self-direction and self-government were the most important lessons to be taught[2] and Mr. Bird held the boys as associates and friends.[3]   Moreover, Mr. Gunn's use of the school as a social center—the reception held on Friday evenings in which girls of the village took part in the games and dancing—are ideas incorporated into the novel.[4]   Thus it was that the high social and intellectual qualities of the village played a large part in the cultural development of the boys—an influence not found in the frontier school.

Shortly after Mr. Gunn's death in 1881 a lament was sent up on the account of "The Disappearance of the Schoolmaster"[5] out of the land as that of Charles Lamb for the "Decay of Beggars in the Metropolis." The old schoolmaster with his genuine interest in the individual child is giving place to systems of education, asserts the writer. The keeper of the "Gunnery" was able to communicate something to his pupils better than mere knowledge.[6]   Such an old schoolmaster was Mr. Bird, and if Mr. Holland gave us an idealized picture of the old New England academy, it was because of the ideal quality of his source. Early critics condemned the book on this score. They thought it lacked imagination, had too many wholesome lessons and too much simplicity,

[1] Ibid., 350.
[2] *Arthur Bonnicastle*, 69.
[3] Ibid., 119.
[4] Ibid., 70.
[5] THE CENTURY MAGAZINE, Vol. I, 17.
[6] Ibid., 618.

but admitted that it had a mission of good which it was bound to fulfill.[1]

Whether the old schoolmaster as such was passing does not primarily concern this study. But one thing is certain—that the term *Schoolmaster* was used with rapidly diminishing frequency in the literature dealing with the school after 1875. *The Hoosier Schoolmaster* (1871) was giving way to *The Hoosier Schoolboy* (1883) and childlife, instead of the lot of the schoolmaster, was taking the stage. In books read by adults during this period the child makes a relatively small figure; in both *Locke Amsden* and *Arthur Bonnicastle* the emphasis is given to the schoolmaster and to educational method. To trace the developing interest in child life at school, we must turn to the children's books of this period—an interest which, too, belongs to the more refined, older communities.

3. THE SCHOOL IN CHILD LITERATURE

By 1830 John Neal had expressed a romantic view of school boys, which reflects the growing interest in but a certain adult aloofness from children:[2]

What are children? Step to the window with me. The street is full of them. Yonder is a school let loose. . . . Here just within reach of our observation are two or three noisy little fellows, and there another party mustering for play. Some are whispering together and plotting so loudly and so earnestly as to attract everybody's attention, while others are holding themselves aloof, with their satchels gaping so as to betray a part of their plans for tomorrow afternoon, of laying their heads together in pairs for a trip to the islands.

[1] OVERLAND MAGAZINE, Vol. XI, 484.
  EDUCATIONAL TIMES (London, 1874), Vol. 27, 16.
[2] From "The Token," reprinted in Griswold's *Prose Writers of America* (London, 1847), 321.

Whittier, introducing his *Child Life in Prose* (Boston, 1847) quotes, beneath a picture of an angel child in black and white, a still more romantic view of childhood from Judd's *Margaret* (Boston, 1845). By this time, a number of children's magazines were begun, which were, as others were added before the end of the century, to make America the leading nation in the production of special books for children.[1]

The leading children's magazines established in the period under discussion were: Mrs. Lydia Child's JUVENILE MISCELLANY and Nathaniel Willis' THE YOUTH'S COMPANION, both in 1827, THE YOUTH'S FRIEND (Philadelphia) 1830, OUR YOUNG FOLKS, 1865, edited by J. T. Trowbridge, "Gail Hamilton," and Lucy Larcom, who added contributions from Aldrich, Whittier, Mrs. Stowe, Elizabeth Stuart Phelps, Lucretia P. Hale, "Sophia May," Olive Thorn, and "Susan Coolidge" to their own. This was merged in 1873 into ST. NICHOLAS, more pretentious and better illustrated than its predecessor or its rivals. Its able editor, Mary Mapes Dodge, the author of books of abiding interest to children, *Hans Brinker* (1865), *Donald and Dorothy* (1883), and *Rhymes and Jingles* (1879), called upon Lucretia P. Hale, Celia Thaxter, Trowbridge, Elizabeth S. Phelps, Charles Dudley Warner, (*Being a Boy*) and Louisa Alcott for the first issue. Louisa Alcott, Trowbridge, Frank R. Stockton, and Bret Harte all became important contributors.

If the subject of this study included the Sunday School, much material might be gleaned from the early juvenile magazines, since they were intended largely for Sunday reading, and since their contributors were usually clergymen, their daughters, or their maidenly sisters. THE YOUTH'S COMPANION, though it had expressly cut loose

[1] *Cambridge History of American Literature*, Vol. II, 401.

from Mather's admonition to keep the day of doom continually in the minds of children and was avowedly non-sectarian, was, nevertheless, devoted to piety, morality, and brotherly love. A prospectus of a typical volume (April 19, 1849, Vol. 22) shows the following divisions: 1. Moral Tales; 2. Religion (Story—"I Want to Be an Angel"); 3. Nursery (with "Parables for Little Girls"); 4. Morality (with a story of a farm school for boys); 5. Benevolence; 6. The Sabbath School; 7. Obituary (with a story of a dying infant scholar who told his mother not to cry for him for he was going to Heaven); 8. Parental (with a story of a sweet child who was accidentally killed on the way to Sunday School). So it was that the Sunday School took precedence over the day school in these early stories. Among the "Infant School Stories" of THE YOUTH'S FRIEND (Feb., 1830, 31) is the account of a little girl who was observed by her mother to remain upstairs so long that she was likely to be late at school. On being asked why she did not come down, the child replied that she must pray to God for a new heart. One other citation shows the prevailing religious interest:[1]

MOTHER. My dear, I heard you read in the last number of THE YOUTH'S FRIEND that it is resolved by the American Sunday School Union, that they will, in reliance upon divine aid, within two years establish a Sunday School in every destitute place in the Mississippi Valley.

HENRY. Yes, Mother, but I do not know exactly where this valley is.

MOTHER. Get your map of the United States, Henry. Find the Allegheny Mountains. Within this tract of country are no less than nine states—Ohio, Kentucky, Indiana, Mississippi, Tennessee, Louisiana, Missouri, Illinois, Alabama, besides parts of Pennsylvania, Virginia and Arkansas Territory. It is supposed that

[1] Ibid., Vol. I, 140–143.

there are in this great country 650,000 children who are of proper age to attend Sunday School.

HENRY.   Are there no Sabbath Schools there now, Mother?

MOTHER.   Yes, but few when compared to the whole number of children; and this in a few years will probably be doubled. . . . In many places they have very few Bibles, tracts, or any other books, and children are growing up in ignorance and sin . . . The American Sunday School Union will send out missionaries to tell them how to keep Sunday School and to take them books; and this will cost a great deal of money."[1]

Stories of day school life did, however, creep into these magazines; at first cautiously and provided a moral could be pointed.   But as the periodicals became secularized, the school became prominent as a factor of interest. In OUR YOUNG FOLKS the theme is abundantly represented, for one of its editors, Trowbridge, was never far from the schoolhouse in his extensive treatment of boy life.   His *Cudjo's Cave* (1864) told of an abolitionist schoolmaster who, while teaching a school in Tennessee, was caught by masked men one night, tarred and feathered, but was assisted to a place of safety by one of his pupils.   At the same time that Trowbridge was running serially his school story of *Jack Hazard and His Fortunes* (1871), he was publishing Elizabeth Kilhan's true stories of negro school children in the South,[2] some of the many stories of the schools established by The Freedman's Bureau during Reconstruction.[3]   "When the combat

[1] NOTE:—In 1835 Rev. Jonathan Farr published his *Sunday School Teacher's Funeral* (Boston) which has been called "one of the most effective bits of writing in the English language."   See Channing, *History of the United States*, Vol. V, 278.

[2] OUR YOUNG FOLKS, "Flibertigibbet" (March, 1871), 150. Also "Freed Children at Washington" (November, 1871), 659.

[3] Hall, *Half Hours in Southern History* (Richmond, 1907), 276–277.

Brinton Elliot, *The Stranger* (N. Y., 1907).

was over and the Yankee school-ma'ams followed in the train of the northern armies, the business of educating the negroes was a continuation of hostilities against the vanquished and was so regarded to a considerable extent on both sides."[1] The missionary "schoolma'am" thus became a kind of tradition in the South, even before the Civil War; but sons of the members of the New England Freedman's Society read these stories of little colored boys at school with a high sense of philanthropy, no doubt.[2]

During the same year (1871) Elizabeth Stuart Phelps (Mrs. Ward) contributes a serial, *The Girl Who Could Not Write a Composition*, a subject which the children considered very difficult.[3] The following year brought another serial from Trowbridge which was a story of a good little girl in a district school, nicknamed "Poverty-Toes," a new "Goody Two Shoes" story by Mrs. S. B. Samuel, a story of a real visit to Rugby by one whose interest in Tom Brown caused him to want to see the setting of the fagging scenes (August, 492–496), and other school stories. The year 1873 brought Trowbridge's most complete school tale, *Doing His Best*. The chapter headings show how close to school life the author keeps: A Schoolhouse Thirty Years Ago, Jack's First Day at School, Treadwell and the Big Boys, How Bryon Dick Kept School, How Jack Got into a Fight, and Master Dick Takes a Hand. The story not only displays a sympathetic knowledge of boy life, but a vast amount of rollicking humor.

---

[1] *Chronicles of America* (Yale Press, 1921), Vol. 32, 211, 196–221.

[2] The Hampton Institute, which was a school established during this period, was to be later ideally portrayed in the story of a negro boy, *Ezekiel* by Lucy Pratt.

[3] Ibid., Vol. VII, 187.

In addition to Trowbridge's stories, OUR YOUNG
FOLKS had the honor of publishing T. B. Aldrich's
The Story of a Bad Boy (1869) which, though the interest
is chiefly in the boy and the story in no way mentions
educational practice or theory, never loses sight of the
school, the schoolmates, and the schoolmaster. The
feeling of the new boy on entering a strange schoolroom
is vividly real: "By degrees I recovered my coolness
and ventured to look around me." His being given the
candy with Cheyenne pepper on it and the loud laugh
of forty-two boys when another read "Abolsom, my
son Abolsom," soon introduces both the reader and the
"Bad Boy" to the school world. There are bullies to
whip, boyish feuds and bonfires in this as in other
school stories, but the author's handling of his material
lifts it above the average. The Don Quixote like attack
upon Miss Gibb's Female Institute (she, a dragon of
watchfulness), his first love for a girl who was soon to
be married, and the cruise of the ill-fated Dolphin are
unforgetably related. It was a forerunner of Warner's
Being a Boy, Howell's *A Boy's Town*, and Garland's
Boy's Life on the Prairie—all books which attempt to
portray the healthy and natural life of boyhood.[1]

More important, however, than the early magazines
in influencing child literature and making the school a
theme in it, was a number of individual serial writers for
children: Samuel Griswold Goodrich (1795–1860), Jacob
Abbott, "Oliver Optic," Rebecca Clark (1833–1906),
("Sophie May"), Sarah Woolsey ("Susan Coolidge"),
Mary P. Smith, Elizabeth Stuart Phelps, and Louisa M.
Alcott. Goodrich[2] says in his *Recollections* that it was
difficult to conceive in 1856 the poverty of books for

[1] THE CRITIC (April, 1881), 98.
[2] Op. cit., Vol. I, 164–74.

children in the early part of the century. The only book he remembers in general use among his companions was *The New England Primer* (p. 165). "Beyond my school books I read almost nothing" (p. 164). When books became available they were full of nonsense or of such shocking lies as "Little Red Riding Hood." He, consequently, set out on the theory of Hannah More that history, natural philosophy, geography, and biography should take the place of fairies. The results were phenomenal in the Peter Parley Books.

Jacob Abbott was, likewise, a great producer of popular informational literature for children, but "the incidental glimpses of life in the Rollo Books are artlessly true of Yankee life in the '40s."[1] Of these perhaps his *Rollo at School* has most of this interest.[2] Mostly a treatise on how a boy should act at school, a good boy being he who does exactly as Miss Mary says, a bad one being alert and active to mischief, the book is, nevertheless, a simple and quiet record of the happenings of daily village school life of that time and place—not a reminiscence. Moreover, there is much sympathetic knowledge of child life, and, were the long instructional passages omitted, it would still be an interesting book for children. There are the swinging on the orchard gate near the school and the building of brushwood wigwams in the orchard; there are stone walls climbed upon when a little boy meets terrifying pigs in the road on the way to school (an incident resulting in a tardy mark); there are farmers with yokes of oxen on the road; there is Julius, the stubborn boy, who throws one's cap up into the apple tree, and

[1] Wendell and Greenough, op. cit., 194.
[2] Last two reprinted by American Book Co., 1903, under title *A Boy on a Farm.*

who always has a dirty slate and does "not appear to improve;" there are afternoon picnics and holidays of watching the *Light Infantry* drill on the common; best of all, there is Miss Mary who is always kind and patient, who plays with the children at recess and dismisses them to hear the organ man in the street, who looks upon "badness as a kind of sickness" and never talks of one child's being worse than another to the entire school. Abbott's real regard for children, his frankness and truthfulness with them is abundantly revealed.[1]   His work is not altogether "dismal trash," as a contemporary remarks,[2] but is seasoned by a respect for children, a belief in homely virtues, and the soundest common sense.

After Goodrich and Abbott had enjoyed unprecedented popularity with their informational stories, hero stories for boys took the field, though the moral is still clearly expressed in them.   This is the period in which the names of Horatio Alger and William Taylor Adams ("Oliver Optic") are prominent.   Optic's *In School and Out* (1863), one of the Woodville Series, and Francis Forrester's *Dick Duncan* (1864), one of the Glen Morris Stories, are tales of mischievous boys who are cured at school.   So eager are the authors to achieve wholesome amusement that the "abominable scrapes" of their bad boys before reform sets in, are far more attractive than their "good angels," and yet the AMERICAN BAPTIST, LADIES REPOSITORY, and NEW YORK CHURCHMAN were incontinent in their praise.[3]   The hero of *Dick Duncan* smokes Old Dinah out of her house by placing a board

---

[1] *A Boy on a Farm*, op. cit., 5–11, Introduction by Lyman Abbott.

[2] *Cambridge History of American Literature*, Vol. II, 400.

[3] Publisher's Advertisement, *Dick Duncan* (N. Y., 1864); *In School and Out* (N. Y., 1863).   Abbott's Rollo is a humble child beside their heroes.

over the chimney,[1] steals delicious strawberries, defies the new schoolmaster and is expelled from school; yet he apologizes, reforms, and wins the archery contest. *In School and Out* is full of stirring incidents. Its hero, Richard Grant, lies, and will not stay home at night; he steals watermelons, and is caught and whipped by the farmer, and avenges this injury by attempting to burn the farmer's barn; is sent to the strict Dunbridge Military Academy on-the-Hudson by way of punishment where he fights his way to the sergeancy of Company "D" and leads his crew to victory in a boat race. Optic's book was a vast step toward secular amusement in school life, and it became a forerunner of the For-the-Honor-of-the-School stories which have flooded the markets since 1875 and threaten to displace the dime novel. Both stories, having Coney Island and the Hudson River in the background, are interesting in that they are set in the environs of New York—a city whose writers have up to recent years been conspicuously inarticulate in regard to school life and childhood. If these books and their like did become the graveyard of child literature, they lived long enough to fertilize new products in hero books for boys.

Another important book in the history of school stories for boys is *Changing Base or What Edward Rice Learnt at School* by William Everett, youngest son of Edward Everett (Boston, 1868). So far as the writer has been able to find out, this is the first school story for boys that deals with baseball as a major activity—and that in the days when the sport was written *base ball*. Cricket and Rugby football were played in Robert Lowell's Episcopal Academy, but there was no mention of the baseball nine as it is known today.

[1] Cf. How the Hoosier Schoolmaster defeated the barring-out.

The game, about as we know it, was first played before the public in Cooperstown, New York, 1839.[1] By 1843 organized baseball clubs—that is, clubs with a coach, manager, and trainer such as that described in *Changing Base* (p. 141) appeared. The first attempt to professionalize baseball came with the organization of the National Association in 1858, the first strictly professional club being the Cincinnati Red Socks which paid its players good salaries. By 1868 the enthusiasm for the sport was running high and in the following year the Cincinnati club made an extensive tour of the country, defeating all comers.[2] In 1871 the National Association of Professional Baseball Players with ten circuits was organized. Between 1860 and 1870 the game fell into very bad repute because of its attendant gambling. But in 1867 a successful effort was made to clean up the sport when over five hundred clubs sent representatives to a meeting in Philadelphia for this purpose—a meeting which demonstrated that baseball had taken a permanent hold upon the popular imagination. From this time on school stories for boys with baseball as a prominent feature became popular, and remained so until football as a school sport took first place.[3]

William Everett, who had graduated with high honors both at Harvard, 1859, and at Trinity College, Cambridge University, 1863, had much of the English love for sportsmanship. In 1864 he was a campaign orator for Abraham Lincoln and was later three times nominated for Congress on the Democratic ticket in Massachusetts. With this he was a Unitarian minister and headmaster of Adam's Academy for Boys, Quincy, Massachusetts.

---

[1] Walter Camp, *How to Play Baseball* (N. Y.), 1–40.

[2] Ibid., 24.

[3] Cf. Stories of Barbour, Vaile, and Camp.

Both his *Changing Base* (1868) and *Double Play* (1870) are stories of preparatory school life. Edward Rice, the hero of the former, learned industry, patience, and endurance at school and, though cliques in opposing secret societies tried to overthrow him, he won the day both for his baseball team and in the classroom, "changing his base" to Harvard after his valedictory. Had the book a little less of Ovid and Greek grammar, it might still be eagerly read by ambitious young baseball fans. *Double Play* deals with Joe Hardy's choice of companions.

"A New Catalogue of Books issued by Carleton, Publisher" (N. Y., 1864) contained (along with the first American edition of Hugo's *Les Miserables*, and four of Balzac's novels, seven of Mary J. Holmes' works and eight of A. S. Roe's) Richard R. Kimball's *Romance of Student Life Abroad* (1853), and *Louie's Last Term at St. Mary's* (1860) by the author of *Rutledge*, "a very powerful novel." Kimball's book went through many editions and was translated into German. Much like William Howitt's *Student Life of Germany* (London, 1841; Philadelphia, 1842), it voices a part of the mid-century enthusiasm among the intellectually ambitious to study in German universities. But when we read the names of Mary J. Holmes, A. S. Roe, and the author of *Rutledge* (Mrs. M. C. Harris, 1834) we can only think of "dismal trash" and the growing pains of native fiction during the Civil War era. *Louie's Last Term at St. Mary's* is, however, with the possible exception of Hannah Foster's *The Preceptress* (1797), the first attempt in America to put a girls' boarding school into romance, and it was the beginning of a long list of such stories. Written presumably for adolescent girls, it smacks too much of the interior of a mid-century convent (Episcopal, Burlington, N. J., where the author was educated) too much of self-abasement and repentance to be read by a normal child. So great was the rage against dime dreadfuls at this school, that one girl, "the heroine," was actually hounded to fever and death because she was suspected of having smuggled a number of them into the school. The story, then, consists of confessions, prayers at chapel, and "how Louie won a heavenly instead of an earthly crown." Child life scarcely enters it, except in one little game of "tag" on the campus while Louie lies dying in the dormitory.

A more life-like child is found in *Dotty Dimple at School* by Sophie May (Rebecca Clark, 1833–1906; Boston, 1864), the fifth of the Dotty Dimple Series, which deals with a vivacious, wilful little girl just old enough to be in school. Of her older sister, Little Prudy, a serial story of whom began the same year, Thomas Wentworth Higginson said: "Genius comes in with 'Little Prudy.'" Compared with her, all other book-children are cold creations of literature; she alone is the real thing. All the quaintness of childhood, its originality, its tenderness and its teasing, its infinite drollery, the serious earnestness of its fun and the naturalness of its play"—are embodied in Little Prudy.[1] Dotty Dimple is just as human as Little Prudy though intended for younger readers. A real child, with humorous flashes of temper that grow out of her school experiences, she stimulates lively thinking on the part of her teachers.

Other books of this period for girls, which seem of perennial interest—as long as school is school and girls are girls—are *Gypsy's Year at the Golden Crescent* by Elizabeth Stuart Phelps,[2] *What Katy Did at School*,

---

[1] From the NORTH AMERICAN REVIEW quoted in Lathrop, Lee and Shephard Co. Catalogue of Books (Boston, 1926), 40.

[2] Later Mrs. Ward (N. Y., 1922) (Boston, 1867); one of the Gypsy Breynton Series.

(Katy Did Series, Boston, 1873–1922), by Sarah Woolsey (Susan Coolidge), and *Jolly Good Times at School* (Boston, 1875–1923, Jolly Good Times Series) by Mary P. Smith (P. Thorne). From time to time chapters from these have been placed in school readers and books of selections for young folk, and the last two books take high rank in the Winnetka Book List, (Chicago, 1926, 140, 151,) being apparently the most popular of the series. The Children's Room at the New York Public Library shows that the Katy book had been taken out thirty times in twenty-four months (May, 1926). Such books as these which have caught the perpetual spirit of youth seem more permanent than novels written for adults, whose tastes are more elusive. Children do not look at the date of copyright before they read.

The first two, being similar in many points, are boarding school experiences for an entire year. They begin with all the confusion that goes into a girl's trunk (*Gypsy*, Chapter I) and end with "Paradise Regained" (*Katy*, Chapter XIII). Gypsy's last evening at home— the happy tea time with griddle cakes to her liking and a mother smiling behind the tea things while father tells his story, and father's prayers at the fireside—is almost more than she can stand; then when the rain on the roof awakens her next morning, she had her first great "sinking sense of loneliness." Katy, on the other hand, has a sister to go with her and she starts to the school as a kind of excursion to Alice's Wonderland. But Gypsy is much more stoical than Katy; she sees more humor in a lonely situation. Gypsy's mysterious secret society, which turned out to be an "eating society," is not unlike Katy's Society for the Suppression of Unladylike Conduct (S. S. U. C.).

On the whole it is the letters from home, the Christmas boxes, the autumn vacations, and the waiting for spring that figure larger in the girls' minds than actual classroom activities. The principals are indulgent and afraid of frightening the pupils away from school, and one of Katy's teachers is soon to be married; therefore, "took no particular pains to mete out justice." Here, again, composition is the bugbear. The subjects handed to Gypsy might well have called forth interjections: The Character of Caesar, Enthusiasm, Destruction of Pompeii, Advantages of Mathematics and other disciplinary subjects, Sorrowing Nature, Marius in the Ruins of Carthage, and Sylvan Scenes. Yet under these circumstances her motto remained: "I won't be a dunce, but I can't be a model." The death of one of her classmates, and the black dress worn by another whose brother has just been killed in the Civil War caused Gypsy, however, to leave the school a sadder but wiser girl. Perhaps this is one reason why she is less popular than the more sprightly Katy.

Other boarding school stories appear at this time, but they, as a whole, lack vitality. *School Days of Beulah Romney* by Julia A. Eastman (N. Y., 1872) is the story of an up-state Vermonter who attends a boarding school in a seaside town near Boston at which the students live with families. There is strong prejudice in this story on the part of the snobbish girls of Boston both against the Vermonter who has trouble with her English and against the Southern girl whom they look upon as given to piety, many kisses and much weeping. But that "the pillow is the schoolgirl's refuge of sorrow" (p. 306) is true of all the students. The Southern girl, who holds prayer-meetings in her room, proves to be guilty of stealing a purse and this gives the student with atheistic tendencies a chance to question all Christianity, conservative and emotional.

The book while full of Mid-Victorian sentimentality—Sundays, Bibles, prayer-meetings, Tennyson's poetry and "pure gold girls"—contains much satire upon Southern emotional religion. *Miss Ashton's Girls* (6 volumes, N. Y., 1874) by Joanna H. Mathews, author of the Bessie Books, is an entire serial based on boarding school life. *The New Scholar*, second of the *Series*, comes nearest to the schoolroom. If, as a contemporary critic remarks, these stories are "perfect models of what books for very young children should be" (AMERICAN BAPTIST, Publisher's Advertisement), they are very far from normal child life in their effort to inculcate morality.

Jolly Good Times at School (1875) takes us out of the cloistered walls of the boarding school with its petty enmities, jealousies, and thieveries, into the open air of a New England district school just before the opening of the Civil War. The little colored girl, Lucretia, who is treated with especial kindness by the teacher, the scene on exhibition day from *Uncle Tom's Cabin* just out (1856), three dog-eared copies of which were owned in District No. 2, the schoolmaster who has taken his carpet-bag and fled to Arkansas, hints naïvely of turbulent times. But this in no way hinders the rollicking play of the children—play which forms the major part of Miss Smith's interpretative reminiscence of school life. She realizes the ennui in summer of indoor study; in winter, the Whittier-like joy of being snow-bound. In summer noses are set bleeding by Snap-the-whip. Dams are built across the brook for a swimming hole, while Pedro, the dog, carries off Teddy's trousers just as the last recess bell is ringing. The portrayal of what the children do in school and out makes it a vitalized retelling of Warren Burton's *District School As It Was*. The forms of punishment and winter sports and the spelling and grammar life within the school reveal little change in the two score years that separate these sketches. Miss Smith is more selective of material as she confines her work to one year, summer and winter, with two teachers, whereas Burton covers many years. Again, where Burton describes, Miss Smith dramatizes; instead of telling that one boy described the process of cider-making in his composition, she gives the actual composition. She, too, is more conscious of the home life of the children; doings at school are reiterated to older brothers and sisters at feeding and milking time.

"Jolly Good Times at School" would be an appropriate title for Louisa M. Alcott's *Little Men; or Life at Plumfield with Jo's Boys*—a book which represents the highest achievement of the period in the portraiture of child and school life in combination. Indeed to call Plumfield a school is a very liberal use of the term; it is a fusion of country life, home life, boarding school, and orphan's home. School life, itself, is toned down until it is almost lost in an atmosphere of the home, of the barnyard, of amateur theatricals, and of huckleberry parties on long summer days such as Thoreau delighted to lead. Books do come into the story, but one feels that Bronson Alcott's transcendental idea of nature as man's teacher permeates the life at Plumfield. Boys are taught thrift, industry, and self-reliance by allowing them to grow crops of their own and to share in the poultry products. Even a hypothetical bad boy is subdued to refinement through arousing in him an interest in entomology as well as through the long-suffering humanity of Uncle Fritz and Aunt Jo.[1] Perhaps self-education and self-trust have never been so delightfully depicted in child literature as by this daughter of "a tedious archangel" (Emerson's

[1] *Little Men* (Boston, 1924), 17.

Journal, Nov. 21, 1841) who never loses faith in the divinity of the individual soul. One sees it in Mr. Bhaer's reversing the usual processes of discipline in dealing with an individual case of falsehood; the culprit is persuaded to whip the kindly master.[1] "The true teacher defends his pupils against his own personal influence; he inspires self-trust."[2]

From what Elizabeth Peabody, who was Alcott's assistant in the Temple School in Boston, tells us[3] of the interior furnishings, and of the methods employed by the master, we may be safe in assuming that Miss Alcott bore her father's early school in mind when writing of Plumfield. In fact, two years after the publication of *Little Men* she acknowledged in a letter to Miss Peabody her endebtedness to her wise and noble father. His schoolroom with its busts of the poets, of Plato, and of the Christ; his departure from the Bostonian tradition of memorizing grammar, geography, and the classics; his insistence on making his pupils feel their own responsibility in the case of discipline; and especially his efforts to relate education to life—all these are reflected in the home school at Plumfield. Miss Alcott's book is a product of both heredity and environment.

Dickens, too, made an indelible impression upon the author of *Little Men*. But he, whose *Little Folk* were widely circulated in America after 1860,[4] was never more capable of entering into the lives and feelings of his children than she. He sometimes burlesques his child characters; she never, though the effect of his humor is

[1] *Little Men*, op. cit., 60–63.

[2] F. H. Willis, *Alcott Memoirs* (Boston, 1915), 49.

[3] *A Record of a School*, Boston, 1835.

[4] See "The Two Daughters" (1862), from *Martin Chuzzelwit* and eleven other groups of Dickens' children printed in Boston, New York, 1860–1862.

very apparent in her work. In this history of a dozen "little men" for six months at Plumfield she has included girls with boys as a charming novelty in boarding school life. Written, as she says (p. 120) with no particular plan or plot, it "gently rambles along to tell some of the pastimes of Jo's Boys." But in this she stays well within her memories of real life. Cricket and football they played, but no female pen, she avers, dare touch these games after the immortal picture of Thomas Hughes (p. 136). Yet a female pen did touch them to life in a book which she enthusiastically admires.[1] A fitting sequel to *Little Women, The Life at Plumfield* has held its place in children's libraries along with her first triumph; even on her return from Italy where it was written, her father met her with placards pinned to the carriage announcing that fifty thousand copies had been sold before its publication.[2] Though the sober critics of the leading adult magazines paid no attention to this little volume it was warmly hailed by the daily press.[3] It was not, however, until after her death (1888) that the full import of her life and work was felt. Numerous articles about her at this time turned public attention, briefly at least, to the possibilities of child life in literature.

In looking back over the development of the school literature in the East during this period we find the rural school both on the frontier and in the older communities, but the school taking a more prominent part in the literature of the towns after the middle of the century is the boarding school for boys and girls which finds,

[1] Harriet Martineau, *The Crofton Boys*, 74.

[2] Belle Moses, *Louisa May Alcott* (N. Y., 1909), 241.

[3] Cf. a half-dozen such reviews as publishers' advertisements in Judd's *Margaret* (Boston, 1871).

especially, its expression in books avowedly for children. Boston, as the seat of the educational renaissance in America, is also the center for the production of school literature. Some of these books were written distinctly to popularize and make prevail the new educational theories; others presented portraits of what a model school should be. Early in the century New England, with Boston as the center, took the lead in exhibiting an interest in books and magazines for children, an interest which she maintains to this day. So much, however, were parents, ministers, and teachers absorbed with their own idea of what children should become that they gave little attention to child life as it is. This life at school came in as a theme in literature through the children's books which appeared at first largely in Boston during the decade following the Civil War. Possibly Dickens, whose use of children as chief characters in fiction was well known on this side of the Atlantic, should be counted among the influences upon the production of school literature. The extent to which child life has attracted the attention of major and minor authors is shown by Whittier's collection of *Child Life in Verse* (Boston, 1871) and *Child Life in Prose* (Boston, 1874). In these collections he drew largely from the work of his contemporaries in America.

B. THE SOUTHERN AND WESTERN FRONTIER

If writers in New York City in the second and third quarter of the century are conspicuously inarticulate in regard to school life and childhood, those of the cities of the Middle Atlantic States were even more so. Boston and other New England towns furnished the setting for this legendry, but memories of childhood in New York seem swallowed up in the adult struggle for existence in an expanding trade center. Frequently school stories got into the gift books and annuals of the '30s and '40s, one of which was *A Legend of the City of Hudson*, and two made their appearance in Philadelphia. James K. Paulding in *The Book of Beauty* (N. Y., 1847) tells how a brisk and pleasant-tongued "Yankee Schoolmaster" from Connecticut invaded New Netherland and, as Irving would say, seduced the light affections of a single damsel from one of the ponderous Dutch gallants.[1] He blames the Dutch women for this typical state of affairs, since they, being new-fangled as apes, are the ones who run after the schoolmaster with his red cheeks, his red waistcoat, and his English. Here, at least, is left a little of the flavor of the city when Ichabod Crane was in his prime. *The Village School* by Richard Penn Smith, one of the favorite contributors to LADY BOOKS,[2] is little more than a sentimental revisiting of the old log schoolhouse remote from populous cities. As in Sarah Orne Jewett's *A Native of Winby*, time has made the returning pupil a stranger in his native community, but he finds the schoolmaster in charge was his schoolmate some forty years ago and learns from him that their old teacher died of a cold by exposing himself after being "overheated by the labor of a severe flagellation" (p. 44). Then he begins a Spoon River-like questioning of the fate of those "who joined the thoughtless amusements of the day," and the "picture presents a vast deal more shade than sunshine." More compressed and artistic but less American is Poe's *William Wilson*,[3] which presents a

[1] *Knickerbocker History* (N. Y., 1865), 227.

[2] THE ATLANTIC SOUVENIR for 1830 (Philadelphia), 41–47, accompanied by a steel engraving by G. B. Ellis of Henry Richter's Painting, "The Village School in an Uproar."

[3] "The Gift," 1840; first published in Burton's GENTLEMEN'S MAGAZINE, September 17, 1809.

picture of the prison-like Elizabethan school in a London suburb which he attended when but seven years of age. The first of his *Tales of Conscience*, it tells how his double, the namesake rival of his school-boy days, undid him and contains the usual terror *motif* along with his power of psychologic insight.   Apparently a quasi-autobiographical story, it has perhaps as much of his gambling experiences at the University of Virginia (Oxford in the story) as of those of the earlier English school.   Since the free school idea was late in coming into Virginia, it is by no means strange that she seemingly had no fiction dedicated to the friends of popular education such as that of Thompson's *Schoolmaster* in Vermont.

In the South and Middle West the educational life which was utilized by the local writers of this period was that which belonged to the frontier and it arose chiefly out of a desire on their part to preserve a record of old pioneer days.   Until 1890, says Pollard,[1] America has never been without a real frontier.   Throughout the nineteenth as well as the seventeenth and the eighteenth century there have always been a number of states in various stages of growth; but as the settlements grew closer, civilization became more intense and the old backwoods characteristics were eventually sloughed off. "Civilized man, cast adrift from society, tends to revert to barbarism."[2]   Culture is a product of cities; the heathen lives on the heath and new ideas move from city to country.   Henry Adams, though he takes his evidence largely from foreign travellers in America— Weld, Bartram, Ashe, Cobbett, and Rochefoucauld— hardly exaggerates the provincial pugnacity and vulgarity of pre-Jacksonian and Jacksonian America, for local

[1] Pollard, *Factors in American History* (N. Y., 1925), 225.

[2] Ibid., 226.

writers of sketches and autobiographies bear witness to
the same conditions.[1] Such were the conditions in
Georgia in the time of Augustus Longstreet and Richard
Malcolm Johnston, and of Indiana and Illinois within
the recollection of Edward Eggleston and James Hall.
If life on the Vermont frontier was crude, the backwoods
of the South and West with its rough and tumble fighting,
horse-swapping, and carousing, seems only a shade
more so, since the Yankee and Southern frontiermen
were brothers under their skins.

The literature of the school was projected upon the
crudeness of this frontier life. The schoolmaster, one
of the village types during the era of localized romance
and the reign of dialect, belongs as a prominent figure
in *Georgia Scenes* (1835), *Georgia Sketches* (1864), and
Hoosier Mosaics (1875). Indeed, wherever a literature
of village life has sprung up—and this is true both in England and America—the schoolmaster and his constituency
are represented as a vital part of the tradition. It is
interesting to note that in the case of three well-known
writers of the South and West, Longstreet, Johnston,
and Eggleston, the stories comprising the educational
life of the time are regarded as their best work.

The earliest of these scene painters and perhaps the
most grimly realistic was Augustus Baldwin Longstreet,[2]
two of whose sketches of middle Georgia were based on
provincial school life—"The Turn Out"[3] and "The
Debating Society."[4] The intimation that he tried to

[1] Adams, *History of the United States*, Vol. I, Popular Characteristics, Chap. II.

[2] *Georgia Scenes* (Harper Brothers, N. Y., 1842, 1846, 1850, 1854,
1857, 1858, 1860, 1884, and 1897).

[3] First published in the Southern Recorder, Milledgeville,
Georgia, December 11, 1833.

[4] State Rights Sentinel (Augusta, March 5, 1835); See Wade,
Augustus Baldwin Longstreet (N. Y., 1924,) 384.

suppress these scenes because he was later ashamed of
them is doubtful,[1] for he felt not only their contribution
to the progress of Southern literature but also their value
as a social record.

An integral part of pioneer life in places where public
education was neglected was the debating society which
has been referred to as the people's lyceum. These
societies, the spelling bee, Sunday School, church—hogs
rooting and rubbing beneath whenever there was a floor,
and men, women, and children restless above—all these
items go into making the school a social center. Venable
calls the seventy-five years following the first Fourth of
July the golden age of the debating society and, it might
be added, of the spelling bee.[2] Spelling as an institution
does not appear to enter into Southern life of this period as
it did into that of the West and the East, but debate was
universally popular and remained so until finally super-
seded by women's clubs and athletics. In many places
there were both adult and juvenile debating societies.[3]
This interest in debate played a great part in the making
of such men as John C. Calhoun and Abraham Lincoln,
an interest which culminated finally in a clash of arms
between the North and the South. In 1842 Lincoln was
debating the question of "The Venomous Worm"
at country schoolhouses.[4] Then in 1856 began the
famous Lincoln-Douglas Debates, which largely determined the course of the coming presidential election. As
late as 1873 Woodrow Wilson eagerly joined one of the

[1] Wade, op. cit., 214.

[2] Venable, *Beginnings of Literary Culture in the Ohio Valley*
(Cincinnati, 1891), 235.

[3] Longstreet, *Master William Mitten* (Macon, 1889), 26, 41.

[4] H. Butterworth, *Boyhood of Lincoln or A Tale of A Tunker
SchoolMaster* (N. Y., 1892), 166, 183.

Cf. also *McGuffey Fourth Reader* (Cincinnati, 1837), 275.

two debating societies at Davidson College which were housed in the most noteworthy buildings upon the campus, the administration building only excepted. These halls with their sedate old furniture attest the seriousness of questions discussed.[1]

When Poe reviewed the *Georgia Scenes* in the SOUTHERN LITERARY MESSENGER (March, 1836), taking each scene individually he bestowed high praise upon all, but, copying out entirely "The Debating Society," he says it was one of the best things he ever read, since it achieves freedom and force without any apparent straining for effect. It is a story of two fun-loving schoolboys, Longstreet and George McDuffie, aged seventeen and twenty-two, who made an attempt to ridicule "very good orators" of the community and even perhaps to satirize the flamboyant oratory of the time by forcing their society to debate upon the idiotic subject: "Whether at public elections the votes of faction should predominate by internal suggestion or the bias of jurisprudence." It was the rule in the society that every member should speak upon the subjects chosen or pay a fine, and the boys, having spent an hour in devising the subject, got it accepted by a swift process of log-rolling before anyone could ask its meaning. All during the week they refused to talk to anyone upon the question and when the night came for the debate manifest alarm sat on the countenances of all but two. Longstreet, fluent and serious, spoke first in a manner so as to confound confusion; McDuffie arose afterwards and promised to clear away the mist, but his speech was only a little less metaphysical. Then when a gentleman of good hard sense was called upon, he could only stammer that he was unable to make head nor tail of it. At last

[1] Baker, op. cit., 74, 75.

the village orator, who had never acknowledged his ignorance of anything, was summoned. He rose, stammered, faltered, spat, and sat down. The judge made the decision by tossing up a knife. If Longstreet really meant this fustian as a satire upon the times—and it seems probable that he did—Poe was doubtless exercising good judgment in calling it "the best of all the sketches."[1]

Debating societies are also represented in the literature of the western frontier. In the *Hoosier Mosaics*,[2] which go back to the '30s and '40s in a southern Indiana community, a pedagogue got into a debate with the "get-up-and-snap" Yankee editor of THE STAR on the subject: "Which has done more for the cause of human liberty, Napoleon or Wellington?"—a subject almost as much above the capacities of the participants as Longstreet's. In this case two village and two rural citizens were the judges and the verdict being split, a rough and tumble fight ensued between town and country, which took sides with the editor and the schoolmaster respectively. The pedagogue foolishly accepted a challenge to continue the debate in THE STAR, a triumph for the editor since everybody would subscribe. The editor quickly threw out a Latin bait for the academician who, after he made a ridiculous translation, suffered a shameful *exposè* for his ignorance even on the night of his final exhibition, and that in the presence of the pretty Louisville girl whom he loved. The "genius of learning," who was a democrat and a "hard-shell" Baptist, fled the country and was never seen more, and the old log academy became a storage for farmer's corn fodder.[3] Thompson's story

[1] *Georgia Scenes, Incidents, etc. in the First Half Century of the Republic*, by a Native Georgian (N. Y., 1842), 135, 145.

[2] Maurice Thompson, *The Pedagogue* (N. Y., 1875), 162–188.

[3] Ibid., 174.

is more burlesque than satire and is less artlessly true
than Longstreet's; his aim being to hold the old pedagogue up to ridicule, he drew his picture with too apparent exaggeration.

Both of these debates took place in the schoolhouse
and were a part of the functioning of the school in the
community. Longstreet's story goes back to his and
McDuffie's experience at Dr. Moses Waddell's famous
Academy in Abbeville District (South Carolina) just
across the Savannah River from Augusta, Georgia.
Judge Hall's statement in his *Romance of Western
History* that the classical school sprang up at once in the
wilderness and "that in rude huts were men teaching not
merely the primer, but expounding the Latin poets and
explaining to future lawyers, legislators and generals
the severe truths or moral and mathematical science,"
is equally true of the South.[1] A law having been passed
in 1792 appropriating a thousand pounds for the endowment of an academy in each county, there were by 1840
one hundred seventy-six academies in Georgia enrolling
about eight thousand students.[2] Though in 1786 a
treaty made with the Creek Indians did not prevent
murderous assaults, yet in 1815 an academy had been
incorporated in the village of Powelton only twenty-five
miles from the Creek territory. It is an interesting
coincidence in the literary history of the school that,
according to Johnston, nearly all of these teachers who
organized academies and led the earliest movements
toward higher education in middle Georgia were not only
New Englanders but many of them were alumni of
Middlebury College, Vermont, Daniel Pierce Thompson's

[1] Quoted in Venable, op. cit., 183, 184.
[2] Duyckinck, op. cit., Vol. II, 76.

alma mater.[1] The missionary who teaches the first Female Institute in Powelton, the Dukesborough of Johnston's Tales, is a young woman from Vermont.[2] The difference between the two frontiers was less marked before 1840 than after the Civil War. Indeed the "yankee" and the "cracker" were so nearly alike as provincial types as to be easily confused.[3]

Dr. Waddell, however, whose school, established in 1804, sent forth a group of distinguished public men who influenced the destiny of the entire South, was from North Carolina. John C. Calhoun, George McDuffie, Gus Longstreet, William H. Crawford, Hugh S. Legeré, George R. Gilmer, and James L. Petigru were some of the future senators and governors who profited by Dr. Waddell's Spartan discipline, "lean living and hard study."[4] Calhoun was able to enter the junior year at Yale and to stand at the head of his class; Longstreet followed in the path of Calhoun entering Yale at a time when President Dwight and the Hartford Wits had brought to it a distinct literary atmosphere.[5] Many years afterwards Longstreet was to put the famous old schoolmaster and his academy into one of his novels, *Master William Mitten*, the story of "A Youth of Brilliant Talents Who was Ruined by Bad Luck."[6]

---

[1] Johnson, "Early Educational Life in Middle Georgia," Report of the Commissioner of Education 1895, 1896, 298, 859, 866. Cf. also *Autobiography of R. M. Johnson* (Washington, D. C., 1900), 24.

[2] Cf. Johnston's *The Majority of Mr. Thomas Watts.*

[3] Wade, op. cit., 55, 56, 165.

[4] "Early Education in the South," United States Educational Report, 1895–96; 289.

Longstreet, *Master William Mitten* (1889), 150.

[5] Wade, op. cit., 36–41.

[6] Macon, 1864.

The boys lived in "huts varying in size from six to sixteen feet square" which they themselves had built at spacious intervals among the trees at a cost of about five dollars each according to location, water-proofing, and chinking. "As a rule the boys would haul their own firewood and build their own fires," but wood was so plentiful, a farmer's "truck wagon" was so easily accessible, and the winter so mild and short that the task of providing wood both for their huts and for the Academy proper was possibly less strenuous than providing fuel for one district school in New England. In summer the chinking was generally removed for ventilation.[1]

In the suburbs of this little school village were "several other buildings of the same kind, erected by literary recluses, we suppose, who could not endure the din of the city at play time. . . . At the head of the street, eastward stood the Academy, differing in nothing from the other buildings but in size. . . . This was the recitation room of Mr. Waddell himself, the prayer room, court room, and general convocation room for all matters concerning the school. It was without seats, and just large enough to contain one hundred fifty students standing erect, close pressed, and leave a circle of six feet diameter at the door for jiggs and cotillions at the teacher's soiree every Monday morning."[2] Dr. Waddell's method was not unlike that of Mr. Bird of The Bird's Nest, but though no doubt as just, he was much more severe in discipline.

Commencement in the old Southern academy finds its best expression in Longstreet.[3] Like the commencement in New England from district school to Harvard,

---

[1] *Master William Mitten* (Macon, 1889), 100, 106.

[2] Longstreet, *Master William Mitten*, op. cit., 100, 102.

[3] Ibid., 186, 192.

it had its examination conducted by the visitors, its speaking for prizes, its performance of dramatic pieces of comedy or farce which, finally, was displaced by the readings of original compositions. At Doctor Waddell's school vast crowds, sometimes two thousand of "the first respectability," came from far and near to attend for several days. Boys gave up their huts to the parents and "doubled up" to sleep wherever they could. There was an air of bustle and change, for the sons of the great planters put off their uniform dress and flaunted colors *turkey-red* and *indigo-blue*. A brush-arbor was constructed under the "stately oaks" of the campus and a stage erected. The speaking began on the third day and John Calhoun, who had once lived with Dr. Waddell and who now, having finished at Yale and the Law School at Litchfield, Connecticut, had begun his vigorous practice in the state (1807), would usually award the prizes. "Young sir," he would say, "the United States *have* an interest in you; and should I live to see you in the prime of life I shall be sorely disappointed if I do not see you the admiration of *them* all." There was much clapping of hands and a "thousand compliments saluted the ears of the boys' mothers, from lips that those ladies knew not."[1]

Such was the higher educational life among the Scotch and Scotch-Irish of the old South. But the schools that found a more vigorous utterance in literature were the primary schools which, shortly after the Revolution, spread over the plantations of Virginia, the Carolinas, and Georgia, and were known as the "old field" schools doubtless because of their location in old wornout fields. Washington, Patrick Henry, Randolph, Jefferson, Monroe, Henry Clay, and even Lincoln in Kentucky, spent

[1] Quoted in Wade, op. cit., 40.

their early days within their rough-hewn walls.[1] They vary widely as to kind and quality from the better sort which the novelist John P. Kennedy includes among his rural sketches of peoples and manners in the Old Dominion[2] to those more typical, perhaps, which Richard Malcolm Johnston describes in *Dukesborough Tales.*

Kennedy's description is typical: "The schoolhouse has been an appendage to *Swallow Barn* ever since the infancy of the last generation. Frank Meriwether has, in his time, extended its usefulness by opening it to the accommodation of his neighbors—so that now a bevy of players are seen, every morning, wending their way across the fields armed with tin kettles in which are deposited their leather-coated apple pies or other store for the day, and which same kettles are generally used, at the decline of the day, as drums or cymbals to signalize their homeward march, or as receptacles of the spoil pilfered from blackberry bushes." The "little empire" was under the dominion of a kindly English parson ("with blood-vessels meandering over his face like rivulets") who lived at the mansion and introduced its owner to a love of folio editions and who often lingered with him in the library of evenings over pipe, bowl, and these leather-backed friends. Once when the parson had gone to sleep, his pipe up-side-down still in his mouth, the negro maid crept in and held a match to the broad superfluous ruffles of his shirt. The parson awoke in great consternation and began to strip himself, not knowing what he was about.

But not all the educational life on the plantation is so romantically portrayed as this, for all along the

[1] AMERICAN EDUCATIONAL MONTHLY, February, 1866; 48, 51.

[2] *Swallow Barn* (Philadelphia, 1832), Chapter on "Pursuits of a Philosopher Schoolmaster."

southern and middle western frontier primary education was worse than farcical, no matter how many laws were enacted for its support. Lincoln's oft-quoted autobiography gives a concise expression to the prevailing condition from Indiana to Georgia. "There were some schools, so-called, but no qualification was ever required of a teacher beyond *readin'*, *writin'*, and *cipherin'* to the rule of three. If a straggler supposed to understand Latin happened to sojourn in the neighborhood, he was looked upon as a wizard. There was absolutely nothing to excite ambition for education." George P. Smith in his *History of Methodism in Georgia and Florida* (Macon, 1877, 205) tells of a schoolmaster who, being turned out, beaten, tied, and smeared with mud, consented to give his "scholars" a treat of a gallon of whiskey which he subsequently drank with them. Another, on being examined for a teaching position and called upon to spell coffee, replied, "K-a-u-g-h-p-h-y." "Well, well," said a citizen, "he's got larning shore, for he's spelled it without usin' a letter that belongs to it. He'll do, don't want to ax any more questions."[1]

James Jaquith, who leaves a record of his teaching in Kentucky and Indiana,[2] said he "had no difficulty except being shut out at Christmas, agreeable to the customs of the country. If I had been acquainted with their customs, I should have resisted them awhile, then treated them with whiskey, and given them from Christmas to New Year's Days." Thus wandering Ichabods, most often lame or eccentric or both, collected what livelihood they could among the pioneers. One whose "gnawing curiosity of soul" prompted him to enquire about a family portrait hanging on the wall and being

[1] Wade, op. cit., 66.
[2] *The History of James Jaquith*, third edition N. P. (1830), 29.

told, replied: "Well! she's a dreadful sober-lookin' old critter, ain't she now!" and noticing a musical instrument in the room, remarked: "Is that a pi-anner? . . . Well! I heard you had one, but I didn't hardly believe it. . . . Just play on it, will you?"[1] Sometimes a female Ichabod appeared at the backswood fireside who "smoked a pipe with greatest gusto, turning ever and anon to spit at the hearth."[2]

The Testimonials of one of these wanderers, doubtless spurious but typical, bore witness that he had taught in Vermont, Pennsylvania, Virginia, New Hampshire, Kentucky and Georgia at places under the designations of Bethel Seminary, Bethesada Institute, Pineville Lyceum, Buckhead Antheneaum, Goosepond Literary Parthenon, Big Lick Acropolis of Letters, and Lickvill Emporium of Literature and Science.[3] He was hired at $150 a year and board, but made off finally with $250 which he had borrowed from his patron and a horse which he had borrowed from a neighbor. Idle, shiftless, keeping one face for the parents and another for the children, and almost all having the rubicund complexion which indicated their addiction to the bottle, they sat upon their ancient thrones of authority and the continual buzz which could often be heard even to the porch of the mansion-house, was the only certain proof that all was well within.[4]

Longstreet gives us a glimpse of an aspect of this southern country school in one of the *Georgia Scenes,*

---

[1] *A New Home—Who'll Follow or Glimpses of Western Life* by Mrs. Mary Clavers, an Actual Settler (Mrs. Caroline M. Kirkland) (Boston, 1839), 301–5.

[2] Ibid., 94, 96.

[3] *Master William Mitten,* op. cit., 47.

[4] Knight, *Public Education in North Carolina* (Boston), 150, 152.

namely, "The Turn Out,"[1] a scene well nigh universal
in frontier school life even up to 1890. Eggleston
incorporates such a scene in the story of the Hoosier
schoolmaster, but in his case the wiry young New
Englander was able to smoke out the backwoodsmen of
Flat Creek by placing a board over the chimney. In
Longstreet's story, which he says is "nothing more than
a fanciful combination of real incidents and characters,"[2]
and which like all the *Scenes* was written "in the hope
that time would bring it to light" because of its truthful
record of the past, the boys barricade themselves at
Eastertide in the old log schoolhouse and demand
a holiday. "Open the door of the Academy," shouted
Michael St. John, the master, . . . "or I'll break it
down." He, of course, wished a holiday as earnestly as
his opponents, but a fair excuse must be furnished the
parents, else his salary would be forfeited. In the tussle
that ensued when the master had beaten in the door with
a fence rail, the boys got the upper hand, but one little
fellow who got too near the recalcitrant master cried:
"Ding his old red-headed skin, to go and kick me right
in my sore belly, where I fell down and raked it, running
after that fellow that cried school-butter." Another
seven-year's darling cracked his heels together and
exclaimed: "By Jingo, Pete Jones, Bill Smith and me can
hold any Sinjin (St. John) that ever trod Georgy grit."[3]

Whether Longstreet's explanation of that challenging
term, "school-butter," is correct is uncertain, but it does
seem probable that the opening line of Pope's *Essay on
Man* contains the same pronunciation of St. John as

---

[1] "The Turn Out," reprinted separately in NATIONAL MAGAZINE,
1852, 62–65.

[2] *Georgia Scenes*, op. cit., preface.

[3] Ibid. 77.

that of the Georgia schoolboys. Frequently the "turn out" was never practiced upon a schoolmaster whom the boys loved and respected, but such a one was not often a recurrent phenomenon. After the Civil War when large numbers of young women began teaching in the rural schools, turn outs became less universal, but the schoolmistress as well as the schoolmaster was expected to treat on holidays.   Her treat was candy; his often had been a jug of whiskey.

Poe in his review of *Georgia Scenes* says[1] that "The Turn Out" was like Miss Edgeworth's *Barring Out*, but it really has no resemblance to her story except in the title. Her story was written to illustrate the evil effects of the gang spirit in a school.   Rebellion in a school must be scotched as a snake, for with Miss Edgeworth obedience is a theme as fervently pronounced as with Thomas Carlyle. Voicing the sentiment of the educational times in England she closes her story by saying, "without obedience to your master, you cannot be educated." Longstreet had no such object in mind, but was relating a simple story of bygone days.

Of all who have given a literary flavor to the old field school and who have expressed most fully the educational life of the rural South, Richard Malcolm Johnston deserves most credit. His Dukesborough[2] long before his death had become a deserted village, but the life he described there gives evidence of its one-time rude virility, and "The Goosepond School,"[3] situated a

---

[1] SOUTHERN LITERARY MESSENGER, March, 1836.

[2] *Georgia Sketches* (Augusta, 1864) *Dukesborough Tales* (Baltimore, 1871).   Appeared intermittently in THE SOUTHERN MAGAZINE from May, 1871 to August, 1872; made known to northern readers by Harper Brothers, 1883.

[3] Ibid., 1–36.

few miles distant, "on the edge of an old field with
original oak and hickory woods on three sides and
on the other a dense pine thicket," has left its imprint
upon the sands of Southern prose. Old Israel Meadows,
fugitive from justice, who taught the school, might, if Irving had told the story, still be seen emerging from the
mouth of the path through the thicket with a bundle of
hickories and heard to shout "Books!" as ragged urchins
who quit their bull-pen, and cornfed-nymphs, who cease
to jump rope, scuttle off to their seats on split logs to
await his quick arrival and the further order of "Go to
studyin'." The bedlam of loud-voiced readers, spellers,
geographers, and arithmeticians broke loose and continued until "Silence!" was commanded at the calling of
the first class.

"There is too much fuss here. I'm going to drap this pin, and
I shall whip every single one of you little boys that don't hear it
when it falls. Thar!"

"I heerd it, Mr. Meadows!" exclaimed simultaneously five or six
little fellows.

"Come up here, you little rascal. You are a liar," said he to
each one. "I never drapped it; I never had nary one to drap.
It just shows what liars you are. Set down and wait awhile, I'll
show you how to tell me lies."[1]

Then follow three episodes in swift and terrible
succession: First the circus scene in which the reading and
spelling classes, after having removed their shoes and
stockings, form a ring about the master in preparation
for the coming torture. Two little boys beg to get into
the circus, knowing a worse fate awaits them for being
left out.[2] The gods are against them, however, and

[1] Ibid., p. 14.

[2] This method of punishment is recalled by Edward Eggleston
from a little volume of "long-forgotten Sketches by Edwin House
of a generation ago." "Some Western Schoolmasters" (SCRIBNER'S
MONTHLY, 1878), 747, 53.

no sooner is the scourging ended than they are ordered to "come up and go to horsin'." This form of punishment in which one boy, prancing and neighing, is ridden by another while the master lays on with all force, has been described elsewhere as a part of frontier school life,[1] but not with the Georgia severity. But if as Johnston suggests, as the Prologue to this story, education is a forced march of bullocks to the drover's shout, the bullocks sometimes mutiny. The climactic scene in which the widow's grown son, who had just learned to read and who has been advanced into geography in order that the master might get the half dollar extra tuition for that subject, is summoned to pay his account of stupidity. His mother has made every sacrifice for him, and he, being a loyal son, has kept his many brutal beatings from her. This morning all along his seven-mile road to school he has studied harder than ever, and when old Meadows called him to punishment, all his strength rose up in rebellion to crush the oppressor. This he very effectively did, while the fight was reflected in the frightened countenances of children. Meadows left the country without collecting further tuition, and the widow wept for the vanishing dreams of education for her son, but gloried in his triumph in a great cause. Such were the grim and rude old times in Georgia, and "The Goosepond School" forms another chapter in the history of the rod not outdone by Winthrop's record of colonial days at Harvard.[2]

Johnston, who wrote before the use of the term realism appeared in literary criticism, believed that an author

---

[1] Venable, *A Buckeye Boyhood* (N. Y., 1897).

[2] For the actual masters of "The Goosepond School" see THE NATIONAL MAGAZINE, Vol. I, 61, 26.

should take "utmost pains in the study of naturalness,[1] and that an artist can create interesting concretes only if he can re-enact scenes from human life." From Dickens, whom he admired and had read aloud to his students at the University of Georgia, he had learned to intermingle the serious and gay. Like his predecessor Longstreet, in whose tradition he followed, he was unable to do without places in conceiving a story[2] and often introduced himself into them by way of verisimilitude. In the middle counties of Georgia he found a great variety of individual characters, and with one or two of these in mind he usually began his stories, not thinking how long they were to be or how ended. This method may be conducive to naturalness, but it gives to his tales a certain meticulousness which, except in rare cases, as in "The Goosepond School," makes them devoid of unification. Into the varied group of individuals attached to the plantation school comes the red-eyed, slattern wife of Josiah Yellowby, Johnston's second teacher, who accompanies her husband to school on an old blind mare, presumably as a body guard.[3] If the sentimentalists have often portrayed the schoolmaster in love, Johnston, the naturalist, shows us for the first time the results of the romance. Yellowby's "little dog Rum and his wife's mare Kate were as I have described them, although what was told of the wife . . . was pure invention."[4]

Though school was not in the old days looked upon as a place for animals, the literature of the school often

[1] Cf. his letter to the editor of THE CRITIC, March 17, 1888, Vol. XII, 126.

[2] *Autobiography of Colonel Richard Malcolm Johnston* (Washington, 1900), 74.

[3] *Dukesborough Tales*, op. cit., 93.

[4] *Autobiography*, op. cit., 17.

presents the dog. In more recent practice teachers make use of goldfish,[1] canaries, frogs and many forms of plant and animal life to arouse interest, but in earlier times while the bear at school formed one of the more interesting pieces of the secular school readers, Mary's little lamb had to linger without until the day's work was done. In the backwoods, however, both the wandering Ichabods and the big boys often brought dogs to school with them that entered greedily into any rising conflict between the two. The young Harvard student who taught the district school at Pigwacket Center in *Elsie Venner* had to use the strong breastplate of his untainted heart to put out the rude country bumpkin and his vicious cur. In Ohio a hard-drinking old schoolmaster kept a "yallah dog, named Crusty, a sneak of a canine that made his living by stealing it with impunity from the lunch baskets behind the door."[2] In *The Hoosier Schoolmaster* a fierce bull-dog was brought to school on the second day and placed as guard at the desk in order to try the teacher's metal. When the tailless Rum, whose earless head peers out between the rounds of the teacher's chair, and the old blind mare are introduced into Johnston's story, one wonders what possible use can be made of them; but as the story moves through its crises, the dog watches with keen interest the growing conflict, and the old white mare is the chief source of the clash between the schoolmaster's wife and the large girl who took unwarranted liberties in riding her at recess time.

In the Goosepond story the grown girls were not spared in the wholesale flogging circuses of Israel Meadows, but

[1] Cf. Myra Kelly, *Little Citizens.*

[2] Alexander Clark, *The Old Log Schoolhouse* (Philadelphia, 1864), 72.

in that of Bill Williams, since boys of all ages were freely beaten, they were frequently called upon to offer their bodies a living sacrifice in the place of incriminated females. This is how it came about that Mr. Bill Williams, one of Johnston's favorite characters, "took upon himself the responsibility"[1] of answering for the Retort Courteous and Reply Churlish of the belle of the school to the schoolmaster and his wife. A fat boy had volunteered in her place once before, but had resolved in the midst of vicarious suffering never to do so again; hence there was nothing for Mr. Bill to do (who had, as all knew, a secret liking for the girl) but to take her sins upon himself. This was further complicated by his own timid indecision which misgave the weak self-importance of his exterior, by the fact that boys with a grudge against the master set him on, and by the fact that the girl did not reciprocate his regard. In his suffering himself to be beaten instead of fighting it out with the master, he lost all chance of the girl's respect.

Johnston's stories representing old school life in Middle Georgia, while their chief interest seems to be centered in the various schoolmasters, consist largely of the conflict between the pedagogues and the older boys. Sometimes this conflict is brought about, as in the case of Bill Williams, by the master's changing his policy from leniency to strictness in the middle of the term. But more often the large boys are stupid, are pitifully helpless at individual study, and care more for "possum and coon hunting" at night with the negroes than for studies. Child life comes in as a background to this conflict. The vivid incident of the part that sorghum molasses played in the life of Southern country boys, of the boring holes in bis-

[1] "How Mr. Bill Williams Takes the Responsibility" Johnston op. cit. See *Dukesborough Tales*, 75–97.

cuits to pour the molasses in at lunch time, and of the ensuing fight between the little boys over the delicacy are only a motive in Mr. Bill's responsibility. The poor widow's son figures largely in the stories, in three of which he is a main character. "The Majority of Mr. Thomas Watts" is a humorous sketch of a widow's adolescent son who, when at fourteen he put off his sister's dresses, falls in love with the young Vermont teacher in the Dukesborough Female Institute, but this being discovered by his mother, he is mercilessly flogged and put back into dresses.

Since, however, Johnston's chief school stories deal with the old field school on his father's plantation, we get the reaction of the same recurrent characters under varying conditions and teachers. "Old Friends and New"[1] presents the school in its most favorable light. The cultured son of a Virginia gentlemen becomes a temporary tutor in the household and keeps the district school as it should be—not as it was. Children brought what miscellaneous books they had and he set them kindly and courteously to their tasks. So great had been the state of nervous fear in which they had lived that they were for some time unable to comprehend the motives of one who laughed and played with them. In this story plantation life is idealized, and commencement at the close of this school takes on the proportions of that in Dr. Waddell's Academy. The brush arbor is erected for the exercises and a barbecue of pig, lamb, chicken, kid, and goose is given by the patrons—a feast which is appropriately followed by the sickly season in which tearful deaths occur. The story as a whole is a strange mixture of realism and sentimentalism in which

[1] THE SOUTHERN LITERARY MAGAZINE, Nov., 1871; reprinted *Dukesborough Tales*, Baltimore, 1871, 133–145.

the effort to make the reader laugh and cry is all too evident.

Very little is said of games and play in these stories dealing with the "old field" school, but in Johnston's later sketch of educational life in ante-bellum Georgia, he describes the sports and recreations at school. Chicks or jacks, hopscotch, chickamy crany crow, blindfold, prisoner's base, hide and seek, hide the switch, old sister Phoebe, Miley Bright, Williamson Trimbletoe, tag, and clapping hands make up the list of games for the girls; and town ball, tip cat, bull pen; socket, jumping, knucks, ring marbles, leapfrog, mumble peg, and lap jacket form the chief games for the boys. But the life that got into Johnston's stories was centered around the struggle with the teacher and with the dull lessons that had to be memorized. It is interesting to note that the books used in these post-revolutionary schools were much the same as those in New England and in the West: *Webster's Spelling Book, Murray's English Reader* and *Murray's Grammar, The Columbian Orator,* and in time *Woodbridge's Universal Geography, The Federal Calculator,* and *Pike's Arithmetic.*

With all their faults Johnston's *Dukesborough Tales* present a more vividly real picture of educational life in Middle Georgia than his essay upon the same subject. Dedicated "To the memories of old times, the grim and rude, but hearty old times in Georgia," they deserve for their humor and faithfulness of portraiture, as one critic suggests,[1] a better fate than has befallen them. If one has the patience to wade through the long accounts of folks and manners told in an unlovely mixture of "nigger" and "cracker" dialect, a plot of some originality may be extracted. Little gift he had, as he admitted,

[1] THE CRITIC, March 17, 1888, 126.

for analysis of character, but his shrewd and genial[1] eye has preserved for the historian perhaps more of value than the more primitive Longstreet. "Coarse and brutal" though he was, he learned in time through the advice of Lanier to prune out the grosser exaggerations and eccentricities of his *Sketches*, and though he fell into neglect after the Baltimore edition, he was able with the rise of the "local-colorist" of the eighties to enjoy a popularity which not only surprised him but made his *Tales* the chief means of his support in his old age.[2]

Pattee says:[3] "Johnston was to the Southern movement what Eggleston was to the Western. The two have many points of resemblance. Both were humorists, but worked in the crude materials of early American life, and both seem to have evolved their methods and their literary ideals very largely from themselves. Neither was an artist. They will live largely because of their fidelity to a vanished area of American life." Though the origin of the term *Hoosier* is not yet determined with certainty, it seems probable that his prototype came from "the long faced, yellow-skinned, sun-bonneted, jeans-clad race that lived and throve in the South before the wah."[4] Both Johnston and Eggleston are best known by the record they have left of one aspect of this race, namely, their primitive efforts toward culture.

Like Georgia, the Indiana that Lincoln knew had many laws favorable to education after 1821, but still up to 1840 she was one of the most backward of the Northern States. In this year out of a population of 988,416, over seventy thousand were reported in the national census of legal

[1] *Autobiography*, 77.

[2] *Autobiography*, 6; cf. also Pattee, *American Short Story* (N. Y., 1923), 276, 277.

[3] *American Literature Since 1870*, 301.

[4] *The Hoosiers* (Meredith Nicholson, N. Y., 1900), 29, 39.

age who could neither read nor write.[1] The proportion
of illiteracy was more than one in seven in Indiana and
Illinois, whereas in the other Northern States it was only
one in forty.[2] The education which was based on
federal land grants without cost to the voters, had
proven anæmic, and it was not until 1850 that
Indiana had any free system of education beyond the
district school.[3] Even then the "poor whites" who had
immigrated from the South to the lower half of the state,
voted a heavy negative to public education.[4]

This was the educational status of the Hoosiers as
Eggleston's schoolmaster found them. But in spite of
this condition Eggleston later wrote, in 1879, doubtless
to mitigate somewhat the unfavorable impression of his
novel, that there was never a period of indifference to
education in the Ohio River region. "So great was the
desire for education in Indiana, even at this early date,
that before my memory of the place (that is, before 1840)
our old town Vevay was adorned by a "County Seminary."[5] He recalls lovingly not only his justly famous
teacher, Mrs. Julia L. Dumont, but a specific incident
of a poor bound boy who rode a farm horse many miles
one cold winter morning to get a master to show him
how to do a sum and offered his last "quarter" for the aid
he received.

[1] AMERICAN JOURNAL OF EDUCATION, Barnard, Vol. 24, 1873,
247, 249, 253, 256.

[2] *The Hoosiers* (Meredith Nicholson, N. Y., 1900), 42, 43;
Education in Indiana, Boone, 87.

[3] *Revised Laws of Indiana* (Corydon, 1824), 379; *Revised Laws of
Indiana* (Indianapolis, 1840), 463; see also *Reports of Commissioner of Education*, 1898–1899, Vol. I, 373–380.

[4] Boone, op. cit., 104; Nicholson, op. cit., 83–86.

[5] "Some Western Schoolmasters," SCRIBNER'S MONTHLY, 1878
1879, 750.

Besides Eggleston there are many whose memories go
back to the actual conditions in the West prior to the
Civil War. Judge James Hall of Illinois, one of the
earliest writers of this region, gives a lavender and lace
treatment for the LADY BOOKS of the romantic love
between "My Cousin Lucy and the Village Teacher."[1]
Yet we get from Hall, maugre his roseate sentimentalism,
perhaps a more truthful account of boarding round than
is found in Irving. When the schoolmaster was a dull
prosaic dog scantily supplied with good manners and good
fellowship, as was usually the case, the week of his
reception, Hall declares, "wore heavily away, the table
was less plentifully spread than usual, and the whiskey
jug was sure to have suffered some disaster on the day
previous to his arrival." Then the head of the family
talked of the effeminacy of learning, the high cost of
schooling, and gave the schoolmaster to understand that
he was tolerated and fed for the purpose of keeping the
children out of mischief.[2] "But if the schoolmaster
was a pleasant fellow, one who read the newspapers,
played the fiddle, and told a good story, the week of his
visitation brought holiday times to the farmer's fireside—
and the cheerful family enjoyed seven long days of good
humor and good eating."[3]

Maurice Thompson's "Pedagogue" is as lean and ill-
favored a genius of learning as any that ever "circulated
articles" in the land of Lincoln and Peter Cartwright,
or as any that Irving or Johnston ever conceived. He
was a Democrat, a hardshell Baptist; poor, virtuous,
happy; awful when applying the rod. Yet withall he
was the intellectual and moral center to whom his

[1] *Soldier's Bride and Other Tales* (Philadelphia, 1833), 56, 81.

[2] Ibid., 64.

[3] Ibid., 65.   "Pedagogue," Maurice Thompson, *Hoosier Mosaics*,
1875, 162, 188.

community looked, "a humble pioneer of American letters, *a character in our national history*."[1]

Caroline Kirkland, whose experience in the West led her to write *The Schoolmaster's Progress*,[2] comes near to both the plot and the spirit of Eggleston's famous story. She, however, bearing in mind her feminine audience, is chiefly interested in the theme of the schoolmaster's progress in love. Into her story, as into Eggleston's, enters the figure of the Eastern girl who had brought with her into the clearing a "variety of city airs and graces" and had condescended to be amused by such rustic merrymakings as the spelling-bee and the exhibition. It was she who retarded the progress of the schoolmaster's love for his best speller and all but shattered the cloud of glory which the schoolmaster labored to leave trailing behind him at commencement. Here, too, are the rude audience with its prejudice against learning, the gravity of the schoolmaster on duty, the mild satire on city manners, and the picture of the schoolmaster as escort on moonlit nights after the spelling bee—all of which figure later in the Indiana legend.

Robert Dudley, whose memory goes back to the time of the appearance in Indiana of *McGuffey's First Reader* (1837), recalls the deep and gloomy forest on the horizon, the "big road" that led away to civilization, the subscription school with its rate of a "dollar a scholar and fifty cents for a half scholar" and the world-old method of the Quaker schoolmaster of precept upon precept.[3] William Dean Howells, born at Martin's Ferry, Ohio, in the same

---

[1] Ibid., 165.

[2] "The Gift, 1856." Republished in her *Western Clearings* (N. Y., 1845).

[3] Dudley, psuedo James Baldwin, *In My Youth* (Bobbs-Merrill, 1914), 16, 341.

year as Eggleston (1837), recalls[1] how, like Tom Sawyer and Aldrich's "Bad Boy," he had frequent attacks of sickness which came on at school time; he remembers the much talk of free and pay schools and how in a free school the teacher whipped as much and as often as he liked. Hall makes the school the setting for a pallid love plot with a moral; Thompson, weaving in a crude love story, makes the school the setting for a riotous debate; Dudley and Howells look back upon the time with the kindly mellowness and wisdom of age. All, however, attest the crudeness of the old times.

George Cary Eggleston, the brother and biographer of the novelist, in *The First of the Hoosiers* (N. Y., 1903) and the *Recollections of a Life-time* (Henry Holt, 1910) says the only schoolhouse he could remember in all that region of Flat Creek was the one a great-uncle had built on the edge of his farm which he used to lend to itinerant schoolmasters who boarded round and augmented their income by teaching schools.   Almost every family had a "bound girl" (or boy), usually an orphan, who became a member of the family, and went to school along with the other children, the law requiring that she be sent to school at least three months each year.[2]   Schools were of two kinds, the "loud" and the "still;" the discipline severe. "On the way to school each morning the master would cut and trim eight or ten beechen 'switches,' as they were called—ox goads would have been a fitter name."[3] He and Edward read well before entering school, for in their home they had "staggered against books in their infancy."   But since the custom was that all were to go

[1] *A Boy's Town* (N. Y., 1890), Chap. IV, "Schools and Teachers."

[2] *The First of the Hoosiers*, op. cit., 31.

[3] Ibid., 38.

through the speller three times, twice on the book and once off, before taking up reading, they didn't get to show their accomplishments at school. Years later he records that Edward said to him one day:

"'I am going to write a three-number story founded upon your experiences at Ricker's Ridge, and call it *The Hoosier Schoolmaster!'* Then he set forth his theory of art, whether with pen or brush, that who ever would do his best work, must choose his subjects from the life that he knows. He cited the Dutch painters and justified his choice what seemed of an unliterary theme involving rude characters and a strange dialect perversion, by references to Lowell's success with *The Biglow Papers.*"[1]

It is, then, to Eggleston's story that one turns as the chief footnote to the history of early education in Indiana. As he became later an historian so at first his greatest interest lay in manners and customs. The school-master's entrance into the "diggins" of Flat Creek; his interview with the trustee, Means; the pointed mono-logues of Old Mrs. Means; the first and second day at school; the lockout; the spelling bee; the spelling book's rank "along side" the Bible, both of which were an educational *sine qua non;* the doctrine of "no lickin', no larnin'" (to which even men of Dr. Johnson's stand-ing have adhered); the schoolmaster's ability to retain his position in the community only by force of brawn—all this is related with a fidelity to backgrounds that cannot be questioned.

The Hoosier schoolmaster himself was, however, far above the cultural level of his community and it is in his fortunes that the author is chiefly interested. He is a bringer of light into the black and swampy forest-land

[1] Ibid., 297.

of Hoopole County; a missionary of a truer religion than that of the Baptist preacher whose ox knoweth his owner. The plot, though having a minor love thread, is the conflict of the master with his environment, and this environment as portrayed, gives the book its permanent value. In the struggle with darkness the master becomes innocently but almost hopelessly involved. Once he almost loses his way, but the old soldier who "*fit* with General Scott," and the superstitious fear of the devil, together with the brawn of the regenerated Bud Means, opened the road for him. Eggleston, the circuit rider, could not quite forget his vocation in this story, though the moral is not too offensively obtruded.

Professor Pattee has very suggestively pointed out the place of Eggleston's novel in American literature,[1] and in the Preface to the Library Edition (N. Y., 1892) Eggleston himself, in giving the history of the story, calls it "the fileleader of a procession of American dialect novels" (p. 6), and claims for it the distinction of being "the first of the dialect stories that depict a life quite beyond New England" (p. 7). Pattee, taking his suggestion of the literary movement from this Preface, (pp. 20–21) places *The Hoosier Schoolmaster* third among the leading influences upon the literature of the period, Bret Harte and the *Pike County Ballads* coming first and second.

During the first year after its publication in HEARTH AND HOME (1871) it appeared in France under the title of *Le Mâitre d'Ecole de Flat Creek*. A Danish and a German edition also shortly appear, and Messrs. Routledge of London published ten thousand copies in cheap binding. Only the Danish publisher asked permission of the

[1] *American Literature Since* 1870, 92–99.

author who, in those piratical days, never received any
return from a foreign publisher. The American sale
amounted to seventy thousand within twenty years, at
which time it was running steadily at an average of three
thousand a year.[1]

The criticism of it was diverse, but favorable in the
New York Tribune and The London Speaker. The
Nation (Vol. XIX, p. 207) and The Atlantic (Vol.
XXIX, pp. 362, 365) scarcely knew what to make of it.
"The rude ugliness of the intermediate West, after the
days of pioneering and before the days of civilization—
the West of horse-thief gangs, of mobs, of protracted
meetings and of extended sprees" is looked upon as
strange material for literature. The Atlantic sees these
worst characteristics of the West as having been inherited
from the slave-holding South out of which the "poor
white emigrated with their vicious squalor." The Flat
Creekers of Hoopole County are of the same "low-down
race" as that of De Forest's *Kate Beaumont* of South
Carolina and the same system was responsible for both.
Now that slavery is gone Flat Creek will soon attain a
high level of culture.

Contemporary critics agree in asserting their belief
in Eggleston's faithful transcript of life. His weakness
lies chiefly in his loose plot construction, and in the
attempted idealization of his characters which comes
out too plainly in the pathetic talk of Little Shocky and
in the overdone piety of Bud Means; but in this he was
following the lead of the great romantic realist of the
period, Charles Dickens, to whom he, as well as Johnston,
was indebted for his method. As in Johnston's stories,
which appeared in Baltimore in the same year (1871), his
characters, too, represent the extremes of individuality

[1] Ibid., 14, 18.

which, with their goodness or badness, make up a common trait of frontier life.

Since *The Hoosier Schoolmaster* became popular before the names of Cable, Harris, Murfree, Page, and Garland were known to the reading public, its influence was doubtless wide.   Other school stories appeared from time to time written in the same literary tradition.   Of these, perhaps, the most memorable as a novel was *Cape Cod Folk* by Sally Pratt McLean (Boston, 1881) in which a girl brought up in the Puritan society of Newton asserts her independence by keeping a rural school among the weather-beaten fishermen on the bleak shores of Cape Cod and, through the school, enters intimately into the narrow, hard lives of these lowly people.   The author's attempt to make the story real aroused a controversy not unlike that occasioned by Eggleston's.

In THE ATLANTIC of May, 1891, Sarah Orne Jewett published "A Native of Winby" which takes as its theme the return to the schoolhouse by one of its sons grown rich, and weaves from it one of the most delightful of all her local-color stories.   The native of Winby expected to be hailed as the grand ideal of the school-children, but found that the children had a life of their own which reckoned little of his achievements. Such sentences as "On the teacher's desk—there was a bunch of May-flowers, beside a dented and bent brass bell, a small Worcester's Dictionary without any cover, and a worn morocco-covered Bible. . . . The primer class settled in apathy of after-recess fatigue, . . . The spring breeze . . . fluttered the primer leaves . . . (and when the native entered) there was hardly a shut mouth in the primer class" . . . all show how well the author knows her material and how vividly she perceives.   Her story is both realistic and tinged with a delicate idealization. William Allen White in his "King of Boyville" (THE REAL ISSUE, Chicago, 1897) and Myra Kelly (1876–1910) "Little Citizens" and "Little Aliens" set new standards for the short story in the study of local color and childlife at school in combination. White treats a boy's first love as revealed in three successive days of Middle-western school life of the nineties, while Myra Kelly shows how a schoolmistress with an endowment of Irish humor and sympathy may find romance and even poetry in the drudgery of teaching little foreigners in a great city.

In the survey of the literature dealing with the school from Irving to Eggleston, it seems that this little world of education, the school, has striven for and found a place among the fixed conventions of our literature. Though the theme has not been productive of the highest results from artistic considerations, yet it is evident that it has furnished both a sidelight upon our educational history and a means to the study of an important phase of child life. In the latter instance the evidence points toward a vast unexplored domain, which awaits somewhat the advance of psychology but which, when discovered more fully, may lead to the bringing of the educational life of the child permanently and artistically into literature. Here is a new frontier for the literary artist, which may replace that of the hardshell schoolmaster who beat the backs of children from the days of John Adams and Andrew Jackson to those of Grover Cleveland. With the coming of younger and more enlightened teachers, this latter educational frontier passed almost entirely from the scene.[1]

Some of the writers of this period were prophets enough to see the coming of a new era in the study of child life;

[1] See Eggleston's *Hoosier Schoolboy* (N. Y., 1883), 102–117.

others were content to record old things as they were or as they remembered them to be—a chief characteristic of those who wrote of school life in the South and the West. Those who were interested in the school as it was found the frontier schoolmaster one of the village types and, therefore, gave him a prominent place in their sketches of this life. Since so large a part of the child's life is spent at school and since his right education is such an important factor in his life, the field is large enough to tax the strength of Chaucer's literary oxen in the ploughing of it. But if science gives years to the study of earthworms, and if insects of wide variety find artistic expression, children, too, should find an increasing interpretation in literature.

Chapter VI

CONCLUSION: THE PRESENT OUTLOOK

During the century following the Revolution, the period with which this study is concluded and the period in which the school became established at least upon the outskirts of American literature, many changes took place in the literary treatment of the school. "Times have changed," wrote Lowell in 1865 of the one-room school, "since the jackets and the trousers used to draw up on one side of the road, and the petticoats on the other, to salute with bow and curtsy the white neckcloth of the parson or the squire, if it chanced to pass during intermission."[1] Literature responded early to the new educational thought and in cases foreshadowed what was to be embodied in actual practice. The old schoolmaster, once a dominant figure, does not stand at the end of the century in limelight; he walks no longer as Gulliver among his little people. The old district school with its narrow curriculum of the three R's, which reached its apotheosis in this period, had, by the end of the century, ceased to be thought of as the alpha and omega of education.

Since the time of Edward Eggleston both the romantic and the realistic treatment of the country school has been on the decline. This seems due partly to the gradual disappearance of the frontier from American life, partly to the fact that the one-room school no longer fully meets the needs of rural folk. As long as a primer,

[1] *Works* (Boston, 1910), Vol. II, 17.

a speller, a reader, an arithmetic and a slate were all the materials used in its curriculum, the rural school could flourish; but with the expansion of the course of study into a half-score branches, the glory and the freshness of the dream seem vanishing.

Attempts have been made, however, in the last fifty years to make the most of the rural situation, and this has been reflected in a series of pedagogical fictions. *The Old Red Schoolhouse* by Elizabeth Floyd (Philadelphia, 1895) is more concerned with getting the large boys to sign the temperance pledge than with educational reform or school life, though temperance itself was a theme in the school life of the time.   That a girl may develop into a successful teacher and yet leave the profession to accept early marriage is revealed in *The Little Schoolmistress* by Cleburne Lee Hayes (Nashville, 1905). In *Jean Mitchel's School* by Angelina Wray (Bloomington, Ill., 1901) and *The Brown Mouse* by Herbert Quick (Indianapolis, 1915) the authors have attempted to show how industrious and ingenious young teachers may transform the life in a rural school and community. Miss Wray, though perhaps over-idealizing children and autumn woods, makes a school year in the country seem as a delightful summer's day of childhood—a day tinged with the sadness at the end not unlike that of Daudet's French schoolmaster who taught his "Last Class" in war-torn Alsace.   Hers is a companion book to Palmer's *Ideal Teacher*.   Herbert Quick attempts more frankly and practically to solve the problem of rural education by showing how a vigorous young man coming up out of his own community may redirect the interests and activities of children toward agricultural life instead of toward the traditional, city-like course of study.   Like Well's *Story of a Great Schoolmaster*, both these books aim at presenting education as life, not merely as a preparation for life.

Less heedful of pedagogy are a number of books on rural school life which still prove attractive to children, yet they contrast abundantly the ways of the old and the new teacher. *The Hoosier Schoolboy* (1883) already mentioned, and *Chronicles of a Country School Teacher* (Barbara Tucker Pugh, Baltimore, 1919), record the happy life of childhood at various Indiana "Punkin Ridges" when a sympathetic and imaginative teacher understands and loves the individuality of children. Mary H. Catherwood in *Rocky Fork*[1] does for a little girl in a central Ohio district what Eggleston did for his Hoosier schoolboy. Reverend Charles W. Gordon (pseud. Ralph Connor) in *Glengary Schooldays* (N. Y., 1902) recounts the plucky life of the sons of sturdy Scotch immigrants which shows their blood relation to the author of *Invictus*—a stamina which, though coming out in the old heroic schooldays when big boys played dangerous games on the ice, was still found characteristic of the Canadian youth of the World War after they had gone to school to a generation of "gurl" teachers. Like Hovey's *Sons of Dartmouth* they had the "still North in their veins, the hill winds in their breath." Strength of character in these sons seems no whit broken by these fathers who could administer relentless floggings under the pall of family prayers.

As late as 1916 Dorothy Canfield emphasizes in *Understood Betsy* the freedom of New England rural school life for a little girl brought up in the repressive atmosphere of a maidenly aunt and a city-graded system where

[1] Cf. *Young Folks' Library in Twenty Volumes* edited by T. B. Aldrich (Boston, 1901). Vol. III, "Stories of School and College Days."

children are "classified and pigeonholed," a theme which Eugene Wood had previously sentimentalized over in the short story, *The Old Red Schoolhouse*.[1] Wood maintained that "the secret of the nation's greatness" lay in the thousands of red schoolhouses that dot the land and in the materials that went into the *McGuffey Readers*.[2]

During the two decades just following the Civil War, when the graded and high school systems were rapidly spreading throughout the North, several educational romances appeared which attracted wide attention in teachers' circles and which still dealt with the old theme of conflict with the private academies but emphasized the application of the new educational ideas. Chief among these were *Roderick Hume* (Chas. W. Bardeen, Syracuse, 1879), *The Schoolmaster's Trial* (A. Perry, N. Y., 1881) and *The Evolution of Dodd* (Wm. H. Smith. N. Y., 1884). To what extent fiction was made to go in educational matters may be illustrated by an attempt to make romance of grammar.[3]

Bardeen, a native of Groton, Massachusetts, and a returned soldier, established a school magazine at Syracuse, New York, in which he became as prolific in school tales and gossip as a garrulous janitor of forty years' experience. *Roderick Hume*, however, has a real

---

[1] McClure's Magazine, February, 1905, 390–401.

[2]   "Oh, the little old red school-house on the hill,
   Oh, the little old red school-house on the hill,
   And my heart with joy o'erflows,
   Like the dewdrop on the rose,
   Thinking of the old red school-house!
    On the hill."

From *The Male Quartet's Compendium*, quoted by Wood, Ibid., 390.

[3] M. L. Nesbitt, *Grammar Land; or Grammar in Fun for Children of Schoolroom-shire* (N. Y., 1878).

plot rising out of the hero's struggles at the Norway Free High School for a year, chief of which was the theft of the examination questions sent out by the Board of Regents. In it, as in the other novels mentioned, a distinct change has come over the books dealing with the teacher's life. The old straight-laced environment with its hand-bell and rigid lines of marching girls and boys has gone the way of brutal discipline with the rod. But in this, school fiction was far in advance of actual general practice in outlying communities. If politics in school boards had been treated long ago by Thompson and others, textbook agents and the companies they represent are now *dramatis personae*. If satire on school boards is old, essay and declamation contests are comparatively new, especially those in which the trustee's daughter competes with an essay filched from *Walden*. The importance of fire drill is now brought home, and forms of the "socialized" recitation have apparently come to stay. Parasitic teachers' agencies, too, have appeared upon the scene. Bardeen's ingenuity at inventing plots of pedagogical stuff within the limits of the schoolroom reminds one of William Sidney Porter's fecundity. His weakness, likewise, lies in his attempts at cleverness and the exaggerated situations.

The Evolution of Dodd, which at first failed because of the word "evolution" in the title, and later achieved a sale, it is asserted, of over a million copies, was written to show that the child is not made to fit the school, but that teachers must deal with children as individuals. In like manner the ordeal of the pedagogue in *The School-master's Trial* was brought about through his unwilling though well-intentioned attempt to comply with the cast-iron routine of a conventional school system. If literature as an art has not gone far in depicting the schoolmaster's life, and if his needs do not yet furnish the most interesting material for the literary artist in America, these themes have at least been persistent in fiction to the present day. A recent story by Benjamin Harrison Chaffee in THE ATLANTIC MONTHLY[1] gives promise of things yet unattempted in this vein. In a democracy the schoolmaster's place has been tending toward that of a sympathetic guide and friend of children. Supervisors and supervision there have been, but the new literature of school life will come from those who know child life intimately from daily contacts and sympathies in the schoolroom and on the playground. Here they will finally learn that there are other causes for the traditional *bad boy* and delinquent than original depravity —disease, ignorance in the home, low intelligence, or malnutrition.[2]

When, during the last fifty years, the interest shifts from the schoolmaster to the child, it shifts from a limited and professional subject to an unlimited and universal one. More people are interested in children and child life than in the schoolmsater and his profession as such. They are concerned with the teacher indirectly, or only as he is related to their children. With the development of the psychological and social interest in child life after 1875, this theme has persisted even into the closest realistic treatment as a motive of absorbing consideration. Some of this work has been a direct outgrowth of children's own demand for "stories that really happened;" some has come from a discovery that child life is a source of permanent enjoyment for adults.[3]

[1] October, 1925, "Mine Own People," 496–503.

[2] Ibid., 499.

[3] Josephine Dodge (Daskam) Bacon's *The Madness of Phillip* (N. Y., 1902), and *Ten to Seventeen* (N. Y., 1908), contain stories that reveal child life from the point of view of the adult with unsurpassed humor.

If this interest began in the magazines for children, and reached high art during the early seventies in the stories of Louisa M. Alcott, it has continued in varied and attractive literary form.   Poetry has been not altogether unmindful of it from Whittier's *In School-Days* to David Morton's *The Schoolboy Reads His Iliad*.   Indeed Whittier himself found a more appropriate classification for his poem along with his *Barefoot Boy* in his *Child Life in Verse* (Boston, 1871) than was used by those who have placed it in anthologies of *vers de société*.   It is the love of two children at school drawn upon a background of the spelling-match and recollected in tranquility. Because of the simple details and concrete treatment of this theme, no less a critic than Mathew Arnold could value it as of "more poetic worth, perhaps, than all the verse of Emerson" (*Essay on Emerson*).   Other versifiers, too, have given pleasing pictures of child life at school, as well as that of the schoolmaster, in a familiar or occasional manner—Holmes, Saxe, George Arnold, Loring, Sherman, Riley, Venable, and Carleton.   Here, for the most part, were a group of "old homestead" poets who in their attempt to reach their country school audiences made many reminiscent rhymes about the spelling school, the schoolmaster, "The Boys of the Old Glee Club," and being "At the Literary."[1]   George Arnold's *Jolly Old Pedagogue* with its lively humor and realism goes far beyond the utterance of mere platitudes of educational history.   Holmes, in a poem for the celebration of the hundredth anniversary of Andover, lovingly recalls his childhood sensations on entering the academy and the peculiar character of his first schoolmaster.[2]   But David Morton has come nearest, perhaps,

[1] Riley, *Poems Here at Home* (Indianapolis, 1893).
[2] *The School Boy* (Boston, 1879).

to school life in poetry since Whittier, in his sonnet of a boy who in the schoolroom lassitude of a spring afternoon nods while reading the story of battles and those "long-warring men" and dreams of tops and marbles in the city square.

Cartoonists, also, have recently taken up the theme of boy life in school days and have added to the tradition of the eternal boy. McCutcheon and Dwiggings[1] seize on moments in school life such as Mark Twain flashed on the screen in *Tom Sawyer*.

And this theme has been carried far into fiction since the days of *Tom Brown at Rugby* by the stories of Owen Johnson, Barbour, Pier, Walter Camp, Dudley, Channon, Quirk, Fuess, Stratemeyer, Heyliger, and numerous others. Far from Charles Lamb's lament for the cruelty of sending youthful sons away from home, writers of children's books have found in the boarding school a realm for satisfying boy and girl scout hunger for the romantic. Parents, teachers, and librarians, more alive than ever before to childish interest, are no longer hostile to these books, for they are coming to realize that adolescent craving for narrative adventure must be satisfied.[2] A children's librarian in Brooklyn told the author that she had known boys to wait all day for Barbour's *Crimson Sweater* or *Making the Nine* to come in and to fight over it when it arrived. Her experience in small towns previous to coming to the city led her to believe that these books were particularly in demand

[1] John T. McCutcheon, *Cartoons—Dog-gone the Luck, Anyway* (N. Y., 1903).

Clare Victor Dwiggins, *School Days* (Harper Bros., 1919).

Cf. also Mark Sullivan, *Our Times*, op. cit., Vol. II, 209.

[2] "Every year parents are inquiring at the library in increasing numbers as to the right book for children of all ages to read or own," THE SPRINGFIELD (MASS.) UNION, Dec. 16, 1926.

from street urchins, who would eagerly enquire for
"another sport book" when one was finished.[1] Perhaps
these boys find in such boarding school romance as
Johnson's Lawrenceville Stories or Dudley's *Following the
Ball*, an excursion into the country combined with all the
thrill of modern athletic contests, while their sisters
enjoy a similar escape from the city in *Frolics at Fairmont*
or *Motor Maids at School*. There are, however, many
stories dealing with the teeming life of large city high
schools such as Gollomb's two *Lincoln High* books, or
the Marjorie Dean High School Series (Pauline Lester,
N. Y., 1914). All these stories illustrate some of the
varied twists in adolescent literature to which the early
boarding school romances, the youthful craving for
adventure, and the changing age have given rise.
Librarians have found it necessary to make a special
catalogue of such school stories, and the *United States
Catalogue* has, since 1912, made a classification of fiction
under this heading.[2] By 1910 publishers' catalogues of
fiction for boys and girls were beginning to show an
astonishing output of these books. This year alone
produced two from Walter Camp portraying school football at its best; one of Channon's best Henley books
showing the difference between English and American
school traditions, sports, and slang; two from Arthur
Stanwood Pier, *Winning His "Y"* and *Crashaw Brothers;*
one from Owen Johnson, *The Varmint;* besides a number
of school stories for girls.

[1] Miss Janette Woolsey, Pratt Institute, Brooklyn, 1926.

[2] The Children's Room of the New York Public Library contained (Feb. 1926) 123 such titles, all but 12 of which were copyrighted after 1900. *The United States Catalogue* listed 120 school
stories in 1912. *The Children's Catalogue* of 4100 books (Minnie E.
Sears, N. Y., 1925) lists 85 such stories, besides 13 baseball and
22 football stories all but nine of which were copyrighted after 1900.

Of these writers Johnson seems best able to depict in literature the tragi-comedies of adolescence, though all of them write far more understandingly of boy life than did the authors of *Anthony Brade* and *Arthur Bonnicastle*. Johnson's four volumes of Lawrenceville Stories (*The Prodigious Hickey, The Varmint, The Tennessee Shad,* and *Skippy Bedelle*) have caused him to be called "the Homer of the American preparatory school" (THE INDEPENDENT, N. Y.). Writing of John Humperdink Stover's (THE VARMINT) and Skippy Bedelle's attainment of wisdom and their sentimental journey from childhood to complete manhood, baffled along the way by contacts with the fair sex and various tough McCarthys, he did for boy life at school what Booth Tarkington in *Seventeen* and *Penrod and Sam* did for it outside of school. If Lawrenceville can tame spoiled boys as Johnson pictures it, American preparatory school boys have no right to be referred to as "soft" in comparison with their English cousins at Eton and Harrow.[1]

Scarcely less deserving is Joseph Gollomb's treatment of the high school as a place to bring boys from childhood to manhood.[2] Born in Russia, a teacher and a journalist in New York, he conceives the high school as the melting pot for America.[3] The fierce struggle a boy orphaned in a great city has in making his way, the problem of juvenile crime and the part the high school can play in its solution, combine to make his books not only attractive to youth but suggestive to adults.[4] Through all these books of boy life the themes of hero-worship and com-

[1] Katherine G. Busbey, *Home Life in America* (N. Y., 1910), 55.

[2] *That Year at Lincoln High* (N. Y., 1921).

[3] *Working through Lincoln High* (N. Y., 1923).

[4] Cf. also Wm. Heyliger, *High Benton* (N. Y., 1919), a story of boy life in a county seat town, written obviously to stimulate boys to remain in high school until they graduate.

raderie are prominent—a comraderie which in Johnson's stories, with their nicknames of Red Dog, Puppy Dog, Butcher Stevens, Cheyenne Baxter, and Butsey White, reminds one of the mining camps of Bret Harte. Johnson's characters are just as typical and individual in school life as Harte's are of camp life. While neither he nor Gollomb come as near to the heart of a boy as the great Italian classic of de Amicis, both write their stories from the inside of the school looking out, not from the outside looking in. Their boys present a pageant of school life. They work and play, are quick to quarrel and quick to forgive; some are courageous, and some are ambitious. They are full of pride at the success of a comrade; envy, too, is in the heart of a boy, but this is portrayed as subordinated to other emotions. The school, which is the setting for this portraiture, seems to make all equal, and in moments of athletic victories they are all friends. One seems a year wiser after reading one of their books of a compressed year of school life. Johnson has a vein of humor which is often lacking in school stories, even in *Tom Brown's School Days*.

Various phases of girlhood are also brought out in the numerous books treating school life of girls in the last half century, and the old themes of girl's boarding schools are continued without much change. *School Girls* by Annie Carey (N. Y., 1881) still keeps up the themes of showing ladylike behavior. *A Girl Graduate* by C. P. Woolley (Boston, 1889) reveals the conflict of a girl, who has learned grammar but whose parents have not, in winning a place in circles where good English is spoken. *May Iverson—Her Book* by Elizabeth Jordan (N. Y., 1904) is the story of a sensitive girl of fourteen in a western convent who has literary aspirations and who thinks *Romeo and Juliet* contains the sum-total of life's philosophy. *Our Convent Days* by Agnes Repplier (Boston, 1905) is hardly more than a lively record of the author's days in school, though it lacks the sentimental reminiscences of earlier autobiographical narratives. In *When Sarah Went to School* (1910) Elsie Singmaster is interested in a little Pennsylvania German girl from the farm who won her way at school in spite of timidity. The busy life in a state normal takes on the proportions of a military training camp, and brings about a temporary breakdown in one so seriously in earnest as Sarah. *The Charm School* (1919) by Alice Duer Miller has the old theme of Robertson's *The Boarding School* carried to its farcical extreme. A young man who inherits a school determines to carry out his ideas of teaching charm to girls and falls a victim to that which he would teach.

But of all books dealing with the school experience of a girl George Madden Martin's *Emmy Lou* (N. Y., 1901) stands first. Mrs. Martin seizes upon the same general salient points of interest in school life as earlier writers, but enters more intimately into the inner life of a child at school than any other writer up to her time. External events are interesting to her only as they are reflected internally in the child mind and spirit, and she has succeeded in making the reader feel the wide gulf between adulthood and childhood. In this school where the punishment takes the form of staying in, the author is more interested in the effect of the great, vacant, silent building and the last slamming door upon the solitary child sitting in her seat than in the whys and wherefores of the detention.

When Emmy Lou is promoted from the grammar grades she finds herself expanding in the abundant freedom of a large city high school. "There is a law in the high school superior to that of the teacher. At the dictates of a gong, classes arise in the face of a teacher's incompleted peroration and depart—as for the pupils, there is no rest for the soles of their feet; a freshman in high school is a mere abecedarian part of an ever moving line which toils weighted with pounds of textbooks up and down the stairways of knowledge, climbing to the mansard heights of Rhetoric, to descend, past doors to which it must later return, to the foundation floor of Ancient History . . . The prose light of common day is breaking into prismatic rays (for Emmy Lou). Into the dusty highway of Ancient History all at once sweeps the pageantry of Mythology—Olympus is just beyond the clouds."[1]

Balladry, song, and romance are the stuff she feeds on, wondering if she, too, be not pretty. Her indecision about retaining her membership in the literary society or in the dancing club, but her final decision for the club when she looks into the mirror, is an unforgetable moment. By the rigorous enforcement of the survival of the fittest the high school brings to Emmy Lou a chance for identity and she emerges into the Sophomore year a personality, Miss Emily Louise MacLauren. Tarkington's Alice Adams, just out of high school, is not more clearly drawn.

Similarly Myra Kelly,[2] disciple of John Dewey, enters into the life of immigrant children down on East Broadway. With the skill of an artist she breaks through the barriers of language, of religious prejudice, and of old Continental traditions to get at the heart of her children and to gain their love and confidence. She

[1] Martin, op. cit., (N. Y., 1926), 227.
[2] *Little Aliens* (N. Y., 1910), and *Little Citizens* (N. Y., 1909). These stories appeared along with Mrs. Daskam's and Mrs. Martin's stories in McClures Magazine, 1900–1906.

becomes an interested listener to childish prattle and each child has some active responsibility in the daily life of the school. Her little citizens stand out as Kipling's children, the boys becoming gallant little knights "doing her uncomprehended bidding and try-ing—at what sacrifice she guessed—to pleasure their liege lady." At the games she had "a little word of special commendation for each of them" and was "gentle and tender with all of them." Indeed so deeply did she win her way into the hearts of the little aliens of Room 18 that on one occasion a rebellion broke out when they were promoted. Room 18 becomes the refuge to which the unmanageable boy is sent and it is the setting of many a tale told with convincing truthfulness. Her stories are brief, swift, pointed and illustrate as does Katherine Mansfield's remarkable story, "Mary" (HAR-PERS, August, 1928) what the short story may accomplish in depicting child life at school.

Though an occasional Sherwood Anderson may stigma-tize the reputed idealism of the schoolmistress in America and an Edgar Lee Masters may see the futility of her labors, still the work of idealizing her profession goes on, this too in spite of her conventional life and the narrow limits of belief and custom to which she is often confined in many American communities. If not the school-master, at least the schoolmistress is abroad, and the twentieth bids fair to become even a greater "children's century" than the nineteenth. And the literature of the school will in the future be concerned more than ever with child life and with the close and intimate study of the child mind. Perhaps as yet no Boswell will arise to narrate the very speech and actions of some child Johnson, as Mr. Watson would wish to see performed[1]

[1] John B. Watson in SATURDAY REVIEW OF LITERATURE, June 6, 1928.

but here truly is an unexplored domain into which such pioneers as Louisa M. Alcott, Mrs. Martin, and Myra Kelly have entered. Drama, in fact, has scarcely touched the field, and yet there are moments of school life which are poignantly dramatic. Such a moment unforgetably is realized in the parting scene between the two English schoolboys in the play, *Young Woodley*, by John Van Druten, one who has just been expelled and the other who is to remain. Again in the story of "Paul's Case," by Willa Cather, a sharply dramatic situation is achieved in Paul's trial before the teachers of the Pittsburgh High School. So far it seems that the short story, because of its seeming demand for brief dramatic moments, has lent itself most readily to the literature of school life.

In the future he who writes the permanent and full record of school life must have lived in the schoolroom and possess a genius for the study and observation of child life. Then he who writes the story of child life at school will do for children what the great novelists of the nineteenth century—Eliot, Meredith, and Hardy— did for the finer shades of adult relationships. Perhaps this story awaits the time when the teacher's load is lifted out of city systems of routine so that, if she has a genius for child observation and appreciation, she may be free to distill into art the life she sees.

INDEX